HOW TO BECOME A PUBLIC SPEAKER

Showing The Best Manner Of Arranging Thought So As To Gain Conciseness, Ease, And Fluency In Speech

William Pittenger

HAWK PRESS

Published by

Hawk Press
4836/24, Ansari Road, Daryaganj
New Delhi – 110 002
Phones: 91-11-23278618, 91-11-43667199
E-mail: thehawkpress@gmail.com
www.thehawkpress.com

ISBN: 978-93-88841-03-0

CONTENTS

CHAPTER I

Can the Art of Speech be Learned?

There is a widespread opinion that all study of the mode of oratory is unmanly, and leads to the substitution of artifice and adornment for simplicity and power. "Let a man have something important to say," it is argued, "and he need not waste his time in trying to find how to say it." So general is this sentiment, that a ministerial acquaintance of the writer's was recently very careful to conceal from his congregation the fact that he was taking a series of lessons in elocution, lest his influence should be diminished.

We may admit that the popular prejudice against the study of eloquence is not without a mixture of reason. It is possible to foster a spurious kind of oratory, which shall be far inferior to the rudest genuine speech. But, on the other hand, it is safe to maintain that every rational power man possesses can be strengthened by judicious cultivation, without in the least impairing its quality. There is no trick in true oratory—no secret magic by which a weak-minded man can become the leader of others stronger and wiser than himself. The great prizes of eloquence cannot be placed in the hands of the ignorant or slothful. But so surely as a raw apprentice can be transformed into a skillful workman, any person possessed of ordinary faculties, who will pay the price in labor, can be made master of the art of ready and forcible public utterance.

The methods of oratorical cultivation presented in this volume are not based upon mere theory. They have been tested in hundreds of instances, and their results are beyond question. A carpenter will assert with perfect assurance, "I guarantee to take an ordinary young man, who will place himself in my hands for a reasonable time, and turn him out a thorough mechanic, master of every part of his trade." The effects of training are as marvelous and as certain in the fields of eloquence.

But this training must necessarily combine practice with theory. To study about great orators and observe their works is not sufficient. Here again, we may take a lesson from the mode in which an apprentice is trained. The master architect does not take his young men to gaze upon finished buildings, and expect them, from mere admiration and architectural fervor, to construct similar works. He would soon find that not one in a hundred had the "mechanical genius" for such an easy triumph. But he takes them into the shop, where work is in progress, places before them some simple task, and from that leads them on, step by step, to more difficult achievements. They learn how to make the separate parts of a house, and afterward how to fit those parts into a complete work. Under this rational mode of instruction the great majority master the whole business placed before them, and the failures are rare exceptions. If similar success does not attend oratorical students, the explanation must be sought, not in the nature of oratory, but in wrong methods of training. Merely reading Cicero and Demosthenes, even in their original tongues, declaiming choice selections, or listening to great orators, will not make any one eloquent, unless indeed he possesses that rare natural genius which rises above all rules and sweeps away every obstacle.

But it must be remembered that there are many degrees of eloquence. The popular conception is somewhat unjust in refusing recognition to those who possess this power in only a fair degree. It is not possible by any mode of training to produce many orators of the very highest type. Such will ever be rare for the same reason that there are but few great poets, generals, or statesmen. But proper education in the art of speech should enable a man to give full, free, and adequate expression to whatever thoughts and feelings he may possess. It may go further, and make him more fruitful in thought, and more intense in feeling, than he could have been in the absence of such education, and he may thus become fairly entitled to the rewards of eloquence without, however, reaching the level of the few great world-orators. The distinction between a good degree of practical, working eloquence, which may be successfully taught to the mass of students, and the very highest development of the same faculty, should always be kept in mind. Even the mightiest genius may be regulated, strengthened, and directed by culture; while moderate talents may, by similar culture, reach a very serviceable degree of efficiency and power.

While these considerations appear almost self-evident, they are not unnecessary. On listening to a true orator—one who, without hesitation, pours forth a stream of well-chosen words, and develops a difficult subject in a clear and masterly manner—we are apt to receive an impression like that made by the operation of a law of nature, or an unerring animal instinct. Does the orator acquire eloquence as the bee learns to construct honey-cells? There is, no doubt, a foundation for eloquence in natural ability, but the analogy is far more close with the human builder, who sees mentally the image of the house he wishes to construct, fits the various timbers and other materials into their places, and works intelligently until his conception is realized. To Jack Cade and his fellows the mysteries of reading and writing "came by nature;" but experience has shown that this much of nature can be developed in the great majority of American children. In the moderate and reasonable meaning of the term, eloquence can be made almost as general as the elements of a common-school education. The child that masters the art of reading, really makes a greater conquest over difficulties, than the average well-educated youth needs to add to the stores he already possesses, in order to attain a good degree of oratorical power. There are, indeed, a few indispensable requisites which will be understood by every person; but the want of these debars a small minority only, and their absence is easily recognized. For all others the path of success lies open. Patient practice in the use of the pen as a servant but not as a master, the study of good models, and the laborious mastery in detail of the separate elements of oratory, will not fail of abundant fruit.

There are two classes of works with which this treatise should not be confounded. It aims to occupy an almost vacant place between manuals of elocution on the one hand, and works of technical instruction in the various oratorical professions, on the other. Both of these classes of books are very useful, and teach indirectly many of the elements of true eloquence. Elocution deals with voice and gesture, which are prime elements in oratory; and although it is popularly supposed to be applicable only to reading and recitation, it is equally serviceable in off-hand speech. Works of the second class give rules for preaching, debating, pleading at the bar, teaching, and all other professions which involve public speech. They show how various kinds of discourses may be constructed, but have few practical directions about the mode of delivery, or that grand and noble work—the development of the oratorical power itself.

This book is written from the standpoint of the student who wishes to wield the golden sceptre of eloquence and is willing to put forth all reasonable efforts to that end. It will aim to guide him into the right path; show him what helps are available, and what discipline is necessary; encourage him in overcoming difficulties, and stimulate him to seek the very highest excellence within the compass of his faculties.

CHAPTER II

The Four Methods of Public Speech
Their Advantages and Disadvantages

"What shall I do?" exclaims the young student who expects soon to face public audiences. "Shall I write out what I have to say, polish it as highly as possible, and then utter this finished product? Or must I take the risk of being able to say nothing at all, in hope of gaining the ease and naturalness of spontaneous speech?"

It must be admitted that the first course indicated above has many advantages, and seems in harmony with the marked tendency of civilization toward division of labor. It is hard to perform several different operations at the same moment. Look how heavily the extempore speaker is burdened. He must think of his subject; arrange his ideas, sentences, and words; remember quotations; originate proper tones and gestures; and keep his attention closely fixed upon his audience. All this he must do with the utmost promptness and regularity, or incur a fearful penalty—that of embarrassment and failure. Few men have the courage to stand long before an audience, waiting for a missing word or idea. To avoid this danger the mind of an extempore speaker must be accustomed to work with the rapidity and precision of a printing-press; otherwise, the appalling danger of failure and ridicule will constantly stare him in the face. It is not wonderful that such perils have made many speakers perpetual slaves of the pen.

But it may be noted that the public reader has an equal number of things to do at the same moment. He must look on the manuscript and recognize the words—a complicated process, which practice has made easy, but which does greatly distract attention. The whole discourse must be brought into mind as really as if extemporized with the difference that now, instead of arising from within, it is brought back from without—a much more difficult achievement. Tones and gestures are also increasingly difficult. The reader will usually wish to give some attention to the audience, which, with manuscript before him, will be far from easy. After he has done his best his hearers will think, "This man is reading, not speaking—giving us what he thought yesterday or last week, not what he is thinking now." Possibly this will not diminish their pleasure, but the sentiment needs to be recognized.

The resource of memorizing the discourse after it has been prepared relieves the eye and lessens the physical distraction, but it throws an additional and very heavy burden upon the mind, and introduces new embarrassments peculiar to itself.

The advice enforced in these pages will be: "Extemporize; take the risk; fail, if necessary" though precautions will be given making failure well nigh impossible; "but in all cases when you speak to the people with the object of convincing or persuading, let it be seen that you speak directly the thoughts and feelings of that very moment."

The two extremes of verbal communication between men are letters, books, or essays, on the one side, and desultory talk on the other. In the one, the pen is everything; in the other, it is not employed at all. Neither mode of address constitutes oratory, but the whole field of this art lies between them.

There are four principal methods of discourse distinguished in reference to the mode of delivery, which we may name as follows:

1. Reading.
2. Recitation.
3. Extemporizing.
4. The composite method.

Of these, the first two have the great advantage of allowing the speaker as much time as may be necessary for the arrangement of the speech down to the minutest detail. Words may be selected with the nicest care, and if the first effort is not satisfactory the speech may be written again and again, until the writer's full power has been utilized. After delivery, the manuscript is at once available for publication or preservation. The first method gives the orator something to lean upon. Should he become embarrassed, he can fix his attention closely upon his writing until he recovers. Should his attention be distracted, and the thread of discourse be broken, it can be taken up again at any point.

In recitation more declamatory fervor is possible than in reading. Gesticulation is less restrained. The speaker need not be confined within the narrow limits of a circle, the centre of which is his manuscript, and the radius the distance at which he can read it.

As an offset, there is the effort, in some cases very considerable, of memorizing; the variable power of memory in different states of health; and the possibility of altogether forgetting the prepared words. It must also be admitted that few men can declaim well. Some have mastered the difficult art, and have won laurels in this way; but their number, especially in the modern world, is comparatively small.

Extemporizing does not exclude the most exhaustive study of a subject. It is easier, indeed, to write upon a subject only partially understood, than to address an audience directly upon the same topic. Neither does this method exclude the most careful pre-arrangement of the thoughts enunciated. The trained speaker will find it comparatively easy to make a plan at a moment's notice which will serve as a basis for discourse; but he will usually be provided with a plan long before he begins to speak. He will aim to understand his subject, make the best arrangement of it in his power, select what is most fitting for his purpose, and then, face to face with his audience, will give them, in a manly way, the outflowing of his mind and heart. It is in this sense alone that the word "extempore" will be used in this volume. We maintain that, so far from being the refuge of ignorance and sloth, extempore speech is often the vehicle of the widest culture and the most extensive knowledge.

The increased attention paid to extempore speech within a few years indicates a hopeful improvement of taste among professional men. The majority of the people have always preferred it. They do not greatly desire of pulpit, platform, or bar, the verbal elaboration favored by written speech; but fervent manner, earnest conviction, and directness are highly prized. Readers and reciters imitate, as far as they can, the manner of spontaneous speech. It is well to remember that this tribute of imitation is never paid by the superior to the inferior.

One argument in favor of extempore delivery has never received due consideration: it is far more healthful than other forms of address.

In the case of men who speak only at long intervals, this consideration may not be weighty; but to others, it involves years of added usefulness, or even life itself.

This superior healthfulness has often been observed, but what is its source? The answer will go far to show why true extempore speech is more persuasive and emotional than any other variety. In chemistry, a law of affinity has long been recognized, according to which substances just set free from combination have greater energy, and are more ready to form new combinations, than ever afterward. In the same way, voice and gesture readily respond to nascent emotion; that is, to emotion aroused for the first time. Every speaker who utters the thought of the moment, if not fettered by bad habits, or paralyzed by fear, will exhibit a perpetual change of position, a variety of muscular movement, and a play of expression which he can never afterward reproduce. The pitch, rate, and force of the voice are controlled in the same effective and almost automatic manner. An ordinary extemporizer, when thoroughly aroused, will employ as great a variety of tones and gestures as a highly trained elocutionist in his most elaborate recitations. Nothing is asserted as to the skill of the combinations, the melody of the voice, or the grace of the action; though even in these the advantage is not always on the side of the elocutionist. But in distributing the effort among all the organs, and in giving that alternate rest and action upon which health and strength depend, the elocutionist may strive in vain to equal the model set him by a good extempore speech. In Western and seaside camp-meetings, speakers who have never spent an hour in vocal drill will often address thousands of people in the open air with an energy of voice and manner that would, if employed over a manuscript by any other than the most accomplished elocutionist, speedily bring all efforts and the speaker himself to an end. But he easily endures the strain because there is that continual change which is the equivalent of rest. Notice some thoroughly excited speaker, trained only in the school of experience—possibly a mere demagogue or popular agitator—at his work. A word shot forth almost as piercing as a steam whistle is followed by a sentence far down the scale, and when emotion demands the same high key again, the organs in that position are fresh for a new ear-piercing effort. There is equal variation in the rate of speech. The whole body joins in the expression of emotion, without the slightest conscious effort, impelled only by the aroused nervous energy which seeks that mode of discharge. When the effort ends, the man is weary, indeed; but with a weariness distributed over the whole body, and without a trace of that exhaustion of brain, throat, or the upper part of the lungs, which has sent many manuscript speakers—clergymen, especially—to untimely graves.

What a difference there is between the preacher who languidly reads his manuscript for twenty-five minutes to a hundred people, and closes the mighty effort with aching head, quivering nerves, and exhausted throat, and the typical camp-meeting orator! The latter works hard, addressing thousands of people for an hour and a half or two hours; but as the stamping foot, the tense arm, the nodding head, the fully expanded lungs, and the swaying body have all taken part, the blood and nervous energy have been sent in due proportion to every organ, and there is no want of balance. The man can repeat the same performances the next day, and continue it, as many itinerants have done, for months together. Similar examples of endurance have often been given in heated political canvasses by orators of the very highest eminence, as well as by others unknown to fame. Difference of cultivation or of earnestness will not suffice to explain the contrast between the two classes of speakers.

The chemical analogy is instructive, and goes far to account for the observed differences. When thought passes out of the mist and shadow of general conceptions into the definite form of words, it has immeasurably greater power to arouse and agitate the mind in which this transformation is made, than it can have when the same words are merely recalled in memory or read from a sheet of paper. When the whole process of expression takes place at once:—the mental glance over the subject; the coinage of thoughts into words and sentences; the utterance of the words as they rise to the lips; the selection of key, inflection, emphasis, gesture:—the man must have a very cold nature, or his theme be very dull, if, with a sympathizing audience before him, the tides of emotion do not begin to swell. But notice how other modes of delivery squander this wealth of emotion. The writer carefully elaborates his language. He is perfectly calm, or if there is any excitement, it is purely intellectual, and the quickened flow of blood is directed only to the brain. When the ardor of composition subsides, and he reviews his pages, the fire seems to have died out of them. While memorizing, or making himself familiar enough with what he has written to read it with effect, he may recall some of the first ardor, but only to have it again subside. When at last he stands up to speak, his production is a thrice-told tale. In but few cases will he feel the full inspiration of his message. If he recites, the effort of memory distracts his attention, and he is probably reading from a page of manuscript presented by his mental vision. If he reads directly, he must take a position to see his paper, and at least part of the time keep his eye fixed upon it. The address is felt to come, notwithstanding all the artifice he can employ, at least as much from the paper as from the man. The most profound culture in reading and declamation only suffices to bring back part of the emotion with which the genuine extemporizer starts.

As bearing upon the subject of the healthfulness of extempore speech, a reference to the writer's own experience may not be improper. Severe and exceptional hardship in the civil war led to a complete break-down in health. The hope of any kind of active work, or even of many months of life, seemed very slight. The question was not so much how to speak best, as how to speak at all. Fortunately, a long series of daily lectures, involving no great intellectual effort, proved that mere talking was not necessarily hurtful. Some elocutionary hints at the right time were also of great value. When the pulpit was entered, greater difficulty arose. A few trials of memorized preaching produced alarming nervous exhaustion. Reading was equally deleterious to throat and voice. One path alone seemed open; and entering upon that with confidence, which eighteen years of experience has only deepened, the writer found that extempore speech was, for him, probably the most healthful of all forms of exercise. It is not likely that one-third of this term of work would have been secured by any other kind of address.

Another important advantage is the saving of time afforded by this mode of speech. The hours otherwise wasted in word-elaboration may be more usefully employed in general studies. The field for an orator's improvement is boundless; but if obliged to fully write a large number of discourses, he must either work very rapidly or very perseveringly to enter far into that field. But if less preparation is given to individual speeches, more time will be available for the improvement of the speaker. Or if he uses the same length of preparation for each discourse in the extempore mode, he can collect and classify a far greater amount of material, and the mental element will thus gain far more than the merely verbal loses.

Only the fourth or composite method of discourse remains for our consideration. At first glance, it seems to combine the advantages of all other methods, and for many minds it possesses great attraction. In it the less important parts of the speech are given off-hand, while passages of especial brilliancy or power are written fully, and either read or recited. Added variety may be given by reading some of these, and declaiming others from memory. A very brilliant and showy discourse may thus be constructed. But the difficulties are also very great. Full success requires a rare combination of desirable qualities. A good verbal memory, the power of composing effective fragments, and of declaiming or reading them well, are not often joined to all the qualities that make a ready and impressive extemporizer. For this reason it usually follows that in composite discourses one of the elements so greatly predominates as to dwarf the others. A manuscript discourse in which an extempore remark or two is interpolated must be classed with written discourses. Neither does extemporizing lose its special character, though some scattered quotations be read or repeated from memory. To pick up a book, in the midst of a speech, and read a theme or argument, or the statement of another's position, does not make the discourse composite in character, unless such reading be the principal part of it. An eloquent speaker on one occasion occupied more than half his time, and produced far more than half his effect, by reciting poems of the author who was the nominal subject of his lecture. The performance would have been more appropriately styled, "Recitations from the poems of ——." The few running comments introduced did not entitle it to be classed as an original production, because they were obviously not its governing motive.

How shall the advantages of extemporizing be secured, while avoiding its dangers? No commendation can be given to those who simply talk to an audience, giving forth only what may happen to be in mind at the moment of delivery. The most pedantic writing and lifeless reading would, as a habit, be preferable to such recklessness. Unwritten speech does not preclude the fullest preparation. The plans advocated in this volume will enable a speaker to gather materials as widely, arrange them as systematically, and hold them as firmly in hand, as if every word was written; while at the same time he may have all the freedom and play of thought, the rush of passion, and the energy of delivery that comes in the happiest moment of out-gushing words. But those who are unwilling to labor may as well lay down the book. We do not profess to teach a process of labor-saving, though much labor will be changed from mechanical to intellectual, and after long experience the total saving may be great. But in the first stages those who have been accustomed to write in full will find that the change involves an increase, rather than a diminution, of work.

CHAPTER III

An Embryo Speech, with Models of Very Simple Plans

The first extemporaneous speeches attempted should be of the simplest character. Too high an ideal formed at the outset may be very harmful by causing needless discouragement. To speak freely in any manner, however rude, until confidence and the power of making every faculty available are acquired, should be the first great object. Many persons are slaves of bad habits through life because they began wrong. Nothing harms an orator more than cultivating his critical taste far beyond his power of ready utterance. There is no necessary relation between the development of the two things. To become a fine word-critic and master of an excellent written style does not imply the power to strike off finely finished sentences at the speed of the tongue; but it does tend to render the speaker dissatisfied with anything below the level of his written performances, and thus checks his fluency. To master the difficult art of written composition first, and strive afterward to gain a similar proficiency in spoken words, is a complete reversal of the natural method, and in all but a few gifted minds puts a premium on failure. An unlettered rustic may speak with perfect ease, because he is not conscious of the numberless verbal blunders he falls into; but if it were possible, by some process of spiritual infusion, to put him in possession of a fine, critical taste, he would be instantly smitten dumb.

The true method is to cultivate the faculty of extemporization side by side with critical judgment. In case that is done, ease and confidence will not be for a moment disturbed. It thus appears that while an extempore speaker can never know too much, it is quite possible for his knowledge and cultivation to advance in the wrong order. The pen will be of perpetual use to the speaker; but his command of it must not increase so rapidly in proportion as to make him ashamed of his tongue.

From this reasoning it follows that the best time to lay the foundation of excellence in speech is very early in life. Speeches made then are necessarily flimsy and rudimentary, but they are not the less valuable on that account. They are to be estimated not for their own worth, but for their results upon the mind producing them. The schoolboy's first "composition" has always been a mark for cheap witticism; but the boy himself regards it with justifiable pride, as the first step in the noble work of putting thought on paper. The same pains and patience applied to the art of public talking as to written composition will produce equal fruit. A few directions intended to aid in overcoming some of the initial difficulties of speech, which may serve as suggestions to teachers as well as helps to solitary students, are here appended. They are purposely made of almost ludicrous crudeness, but will not, it is trusted, be less serviceable on that account; for it is not so important to aid the mature speaker in giving the last fine strokes of genius to a masterly oration, as it is to stimulate and guide beginners in their first stammering utterances.

The simplest oration or formal address that can be constructed has three distinct parts. With these we will begin the great work of division and arrangement. They may be named as follows:

1. The Introduction.
2. The Discussion.
3. The Conclusion.

On this framework a speech-plan can be constructed simple enough for any child. And it is at the same time true that even a child, with such a plan, might speak appropriately who would otherwise not be able to begin at all.

We will consider these three parts in their order.

The introduction is at once important and embarrassing. First words are nearly always heard attentively, and they do much to determine the degree of attention that will be bestowed on the remainder of the speech. The young speaker should select something as an introduction upon which his mind can fasten, instead of dwelling upon the frightful generality of the naked theme. Neither is it hard to construct a good introduction if a few plain directions are heeded, which will be more fully given in a succeeding chapter. All persons feel the need of some kind of a formal opening, and therefore often begin with an apology—the very worst form of an introduction, because it is not interesting in itself and does not lead up to the subject.

In rudimentary speech, which we are now considering, the introduction should be simple, and, above everything else, easy for the speaker to comprehend and remember. If there is anything in the whole world which he is sure he can talk about for a few moments, and which can be made to have a moderate degree of connection with his subject, let that be chosen for an opening. If it is also vivid and striking in itself, and familiar to the audience, so much the better; but this quality should not be insisted upon in these first attempts.

When the introductory topic is selected it should be turned over in the mind until the speaker knows just what he is going to say about it. This process will have a wonderfully quieting effect upon his nerves. He has fairly mastered something, and knows that at all events he can begin his speech. It is well to make a note of this introduction in a few simple words which will strongly fasten themselves in the memory. No effort toward elaboration should be made, for that would naturally lead to a memorized introduction, and either require the whole speech to be written, or produce a painful and difficult transition.

The discussion deals directly with the subject or central idea of the discourse. Here a clear statement of at least one thought which the speaker can fully grasp should be made. The pen (or pencil) may be used in preparation without impropriety. If but one idea is thought of, let that be written in the fewest and strongest words at the student's command. While doing this it is likely that another and related thought will spring into mind which can be treated in the same manner. With diligent students there may even be a danger of getting down too many seed-thoughts. But that contingency is provided for in the chapters on the fully developed plan, and needs no further notice at this time.

When this central division is completely wrought out, two other points claim attention. How shall the transition be made from the introduction to the discussion? A little reflection will show how to glide from one to the other, and that process should be conned over, without writing, until it is well understood. It is wonderful how many outlines of ideas the memory will retain without feeling burdened; and this power of retention grows enormously through exercise.

After this, the mode of gliding from the discussion to the conclusion may be treated in the same manner, and with equal profit. The conclusion itself is scarcely less material than the introduction; but there is much less range of choice in the manner of closing than in that of beginning. The subject is before the audience, and any wide departure from it seems like the beginning of a new speech—something not usually well received. There is this distinction between the relative value of introduction and conclusion: a good introduction adds most to a speaker's ease, confidence, and power during the moment of speech; but a good conclusion leaves the deepest permanent impression upon the audience. It is usually remembered longer than any other part of the address.

When a discourse has been prepared in this simple manner it has virtually five parts—three written and two held in memory. From such an outline it is far more easy to make an address than from the bare announcement of a theme. It is true that all these parts may be formed and held in mind without ever making a pen-stroke. A practiced orator will do this, in a moment, when unexpectedly called upon; or he may only forecast the introduction and trust to finding the plan as fast as it is needed. But in this he is no model for imitation by beginners. Even powerful orators sometimes spoil the whole effect of a good address by an unfortunate mode of closing. They may forget to close in time—a grievous fault!—or may finish with some weak thought or extravagant proposition, by which the whole speech is mainly judged and all its good points neutralized. The construction of even as simple a plan as here indicated would have more than double the effect of many speeches made by great men.

A few simple and rude plans are annexed. No merit is sought for in any one of them beyond making plain the method recommended.

PLANS OF SPEECHES

EXAMPLE FIRST

Subject.—Chinese Emigration to America.

Introduction.—The number of emigrants to our country and the nations they represent.

[A totally different and more effective introduction might be the description of a group of Chinese as seen by the speaker.]

Discussion.—The nature, amount, and present effect of Chinese emigration.

[It is possible for the speaker in his introduction to foreshadow the position he expects to maintain in his speech; or he may make a colorless introduction and reserve his opinion for the discussion. The material under this head is unlimited. It is only necessary from the oratorical standpoint that the speaker should determine what course to take, and then carefully think out in advance or read—for history and statistics cannot be improvised—all about that which he intends to use. When he can tell it all over easily to himself he may reasonably feel assured of his ability to tell it to others. The various arguments should be weighed and the best selected. That which most naturally connects with the introduction should be firmly fixed in the mind as the first, that it may form the bridge from the one part to the other.]

Conclusion.—Results of policy advocated, either predicted, described, or shown to be probable. Mode of remedying evils that might be apprehended from that policy.

[In the conclusion the speaker may take upon himself the character of a prophet, poet, or logician. He may predict results and let the statement make its own impression. He may put all emphasis upon a vivid painting of the future colored by the views he advocates; or he may sum up his reasons, deduce consequences, and weigh alternatives. The choice between these different modes may be made instinctively, or it may require considerable mental effort, but when made, the best mode of transition will be very easily found.]

In all this process, which in the case of undisciplined speakers may extend over many days of hard work, the pen may be used freely, making copious notes of facts and arguments. After enough has been accumulated and put in such shape that the speaker can easily look over the entire field, he is ready for another process—that of simplifying his plan. Rough and copious notes brought with him to the platform would only be a source of embarrassment. But the germ of his ideas, which are now familiar, can be put into very small compass. Perhaps the following would recall everything in the preceding outline:

The Chinese Question

1. Experience.
2. Arguments.
3. Results.

But it is clear that a skeleton containing only three words need not be kept in view. The whole outline of the speech will therefore be in the mind. If numerous figures or citations from authorities are employed, they may be classified and read from books or notes, as needed. Such reading in no way detracts from the extemporaneous character of the address, though if too numerous they tend to damp oratorical fire and break the unity of discourse. One who has had no personal experience, or who has not carefully observed the methods of other speakers, can scarcely imagine how much a simple outline, such as here suggested, accomplishes in removing the confusion, fear, and hesitation which characterize beginners.

Another specimen, not of controversial character, is subjoined.

EXAMPLE SECOND

Subject.—The Ocean.

Introduction.—The vastness of the ocean. No one person has seen more than a small part of it. Power evidenced by storm and shipwrecks.

Discussion.—Five great divisions of the ocean. Use in nature, watering and tempering the land; in commerce, as a highway; in history, by dividing and uniting nations; its mystery, etc.

Conclusion.—Proof of the Creator's power and wisdom found in the ocean.

The Same Plan Condensed.

Subject.—The Ocean.

1. Vastness and Power.
2. Parts, Use, and Mystery.
3. Evidence.

Dean Swift's Sermon.

This eccentric clergyman once preached a sermon shorter than its own text, yet having all the three parts of which we have spoken. The text was Prov. xix, 20: "He that pitieth the poor lendeth to the Lord; and that which he hath given will He pay him again."

The sermon was:

"Brethren, you hear the condition; if you like the security, down with the dust."

The collection is said to have been munificent.

In this short sermon the text with the word "Brethren" constitutes the introduction; the phrase, "you hear the condition," is a good transition to the discussion contained in the next member, "if you like the security," which assumes the truth of the text, makes its general declarations present and personal, and prepares the way for the forcible and practical, if not very elegant, conclusion, "down with the dust."

Among the many speeches found in Shakespeare, the existence of these three essential parts may easily be noted. The funeral speeches over the dead body of Julius Cæsar afford an excellent example. The merit of the orations of Brutus and Antony are very unequal, but both are instructive. We will analyze them in turn.

Brutus speaks first. He shows his want of appreciation of the true nature of persuasive eloquence by declaring that this will be an advantage. His introduction is also too long and elaborate for the work he has in hand. The central thought with which he opens is in substance, "I am worthy of your closest attention." This cannot be considered a fortunate beginning, and it would have been fatal for any one less highly esteemed by the people than "the well-beloved Brutus." He says:

Brutus' Speech.

"Romans, countrymen, and lovers! hear me for my cause, and be silent that you may hear; believe me for mine honor, and have respect to mine honor that you may believe; censure me in your wisdom and awake your senses that you may the better judge."

This introduction is a master-piece of Shakespeare's art, because it pictures so well the character of Brutus in his dignity and blind self-confidence; but for Brutus it is unfortunate, because it puts him on the defensive and makes the people his judges. He must now plead well, or they will condemn him.

In the discussion the thought simply is, "I was Cæsar's friend, and therefore you may well believe that I would not have killed him if he had not deserved death because of his ambition." This is the whole argument, and it is weak because it does not prove the ambition of Cæsar, or show that ambition on Cæsar's part was a crime which Brutus had a right to punish with death. The antithetic sentences lack both logic and passion. As they touch neither head nor heart, they can have but slight and momentary effect. Notice the discussion as an example of fine words which do not serve their purpose.

"If there be any in this assembly, any dear friend of Cæsar's, to him I say that Brutus' love to Cæsar was no less than his. If, then, that friend demand why Brutus rose against Cæsar, this is my answer: Not that I loved Cæsar less, but that I loved Rome more. Had you rather Cæsar were living, and die all slaves, than that Cæsar were dead, to live all freemen? As Cæsar loved me, I weep for him; as he was fortunate, I rejoice at it; as he was valiant, I honor him; but as he was ambitious, I slew him. There are tears for his love, joy for his fortune, honor for his valor, and death for his ambition. Who is here so base that would be a bondman? If any, speak; for him have I offended. Who is here so rude, that would not be a Roman? If any, speak; for him have I offended. Who is here so vile that will not love his country? If any, speak; for him have I offended. I pause for a reply."

As several citizens cry out, "None, Brutus, none," he passes to the conclusion, which is as weak as the discussion.

"Then none have I offended. I have done no more to Cæsar, than you shall do to Brutus. As I slew my best lover for the good of Rome,

I have the same dagger for myself, when it shall please my country to need my death."

He has gained nothing by the whole speech, save the knowledge that none of the citizens present care at that time to impeach him for his crime; but their minds were open to other influences. Shakespeare thus shows how an able man might use all his powers in the perfection of oratorical and rhetorical forms, without producing a great or effective speech. Antony now comes forward. Behold the contrast!

Antony's Speech

The introduction is like and unlike that of Brutus. The same three titles are used; the same call for attention. But there is no repetition, no egotism, no elaboration. The introduction is short, calling attention to his ostensible purpose, and prepares for a beautiful transition to the discussion.

Introduction.

"Friends, Romans, countrymen, lend me your ears.

I come to bury Cæsar, not to praise him."

There is not a superfluous word. But how can Antony glide into those praises of Cæsar, which he has disclaimed, but which are necessary to his purpose? The next sentence solves the question:

"The evil that men do lives after them;

The good is oft interred with their bones;

So let it be with Cæsar."

This leads most naturally to the thought of the discussion, which is, "No event of Cæsar's life shows guilty ambition; but many do reveal love to the people and care for the general welfare. He should, therefore, be mourned, and—the next word is not supplied by the orator, but forced from the hearts of the people—avenged!" We quote a few only of the well-known words:

The Discussion

"The noble Brutus

Hath told you Cæsar was ambitious;

If it were so, it were a grievous fault,

And grievously hath Cæsar answered it.

Here, under leave of Brutus and the rest,
(For Brutus is an honorable man,
So are they all, all honorable men,)
Come I to speak in Cæsar's funeral.
He was my friend, faithful and just to me;
But Brutus says he was ambitious,
And Brutus is an honorable man.
He hath brought many captives home to Rome,
Whose ransom did the general coffers fill.
Did this in Cæsar seem ambitious?
When that the poor hath cried Cæsar hath wept.
Ambition should be made of sterner stuff.
Yet Brutus says he was ambitious,
And Brutus is an honorable man.
You all did see, that, on the Lupercal,
I thrice presented him a kingly crown,
Which he did thrice refuse. Was this ambition?"

The strongest argument against belief in guilty ambition on the part of Cæsar and in favor of punishing his murderers is reserved by the subtle Antony for the last, and then he manages to have the people demand it of him. He proceeds very naturally and effectively from the rent robe and the bleeding body to the will of Cæsar. This instrument gave the Romans each a large donation in money, and bestowed upon them collectively "his walks, his private arbors, and new-planted orchards" as a public park. The argument was irresistible, and needed no elaboration. If his death was avenged as a murder, the will would be valid; otherwise, it would be set aside, and his estate confiscated by the conspirators. The people, thus fired by the strongest motives of gratitude and interest themselves supply the conclusion, and Brutus had to fly for his life.

The whole speech is worth study as an exhibition of almost perfect eloquence. Shakespeare meant to draw in Brutus the picture of a scholar coming before the people with fine words, and producing little more than a literary effect. In Antony he pictures the true orator in the plentitude of his power, to whom words are but servants in accomplishing his purpose of persuading and inflaming the people. The one speech reads as if it might have been written out in the closet and memorized; the other gushes from the heart of the speaker as he watches the sea of upturned faces, adapting his words with exquisite skill to suit and swell the passions written there.

CHAPTER IV

Initial Fear and how to Overcome it

However numerous and varied may be the classes of those who contemplate extempore speech, they are all confronted by one common difficulty. Whether a boy makes his maiden effort, or a man of wide thought and ripe culture attempts for the first time to dispense with the manuscript in which he has trusted through years of successful public speech, the fear of failing looms up before each of them in a manner equally formidable.

The writer well remembers his first boyish venture into this arena of peril. A debate in a village shoemaker's shop furnished the occasion. Two or three "speakers" were ranged on a side, and the question was that time-honored controversy of country lyceums—the comparative magnitude of the wrongs suffered by the Indians and the Negroes at the hands of the American Government. Which side the writer was on, or what arguments were used, has long since been forgotten, but the palpitating heart, the terrible suspense, as one after another of the preceding speakers made his remarks and brought the terrible moment of facing the audience nearer, can never cease to be remembered. When at last called out by the voice of the presiding officer, I found my way to the end of a rude bench or counter that ran partly across the room, leaned upon it, shut my eyes, and began to talk. How hoarse and hollow the sound that followed! All that was uttered was instantly forgotten by the speaker, for one terrible thought dominated every other—a speech was being made! My head whirled, every nerve tingled, and a confused, roaring sound filled my ears, while I most heartily repented of allowing myself to be persuaded into such a frightful position. A great dread stared at me from the end of each sentence—that of finding nothing more to say and being obliged to sit down amid the ridicule of neighbors and school-fellows. When at length the agony was over, and opening my eyes, I dropped into a seat, a striking revulsion of feeling occurred. This rose to the height of joy and triumph when I learned that "the speech" had actually been ten minutes long. It was a grand achievement!

In all sober earnest, I estimate that this first effort was probably the most profitable of my life, because it was a beginning in the right direction. Weeks of preparation preceded the momentous effort, and in some kind of a way the result had been poured upon the audience. From that time the writer was numbered among the village debaters and shared in the advantages of the village Lyceum—a capital means of improvement. Had the first extemporaneous effort been made later in life, the shrinking and terror, would probably have been even greater.

While no way has been discovered of altogether preventing the initial fear that attends extemporaneous speech by the unpracticed orator, yet it may be greatly lessened and more rapid and perfect control of it obtained by heeding a few simple suggestions. Some serviceable expedients have already been pointed out, and will here only be referred to. As simple a plan as that described in the last chapter, with lengthened meditation on each part, will give the mind of the speaker something to do aside from dwelling upon his own danger. He should also prepare far more matter than can possibly be used—so much that in the simplest and baldest statement it will fill a respectable period of time. He need not be careful as to how he speaks, or in how many forms he repeats the same idea. Originality, also, may safely be neglected. The object is not to talk especially well, or to utter that which has never been uttered before, but only to keep on talking until self-possession and the mastery of every faculty have been fully restored. This preparation of great quantities of material with no care as to the graces of delivery may expose the speaker in time to another peril—that of being tedious and wearisome; but this is not the source of the initial fear with which we are now dealing, and when it becomes a real evil there are effectual means of guarding against it.

A further direction is that the mode of introduction be very firmly fixed in the mind. This wonderfully calms the speaker. He knows that he can begin even if he never gets any further; and by the time the introduction is passed, if the man possesses any natural aptitude for speech, his mind will in all ordinary cases have recovered its equilibrium, and be ready to devise and direct everything that follows.

The plan and the full notes which have been made should also be kept within easy reach, or even in the hand—not with the intention of using them, for that is the very thing to be avoided, but that the speaker, by knowing that they can be referred to in an emergency, may be guarded against "stage fright." He may also exercise self-control by not looking at them unless absolutely driven to it.

The object of first efforts—even for the orator who is great in other modes of delivery—is not to make a great or admired speech, but only to get through the ordeal without disgrace or failure. Quality must be sought later. To get any reasonable quantity of speech at first, to satisfy yourself that you can both think and talk when on your feet, is achievement enough.

One caution may be offered to the man possessing a good written style which the boy will not need. Do not make your preparation so minutely or verbally that the very words linger in your memory. If you do, one of two things will probably happen: either you will recite a memorized speech, which, however fine in itself, will contribute nothing to the object of learning to speak extemporaneously, or the fine fragments of remembered diction that flood in your mind will be so out of harmony with the words spontaneously evolved as to produce a continual series of jars and discords noticeable to every one, and to none more painfully than to yourself. The writer once listened to a speech of this mixed character, in which the orator would soar for a time on the wings of most excellent words, and then drop down to his ordinary and very meagre vocabulary. So frequent and unexpected were these transitions that the orator's progress suggested nothing so much as traveling over one of those western corduroy roads, where the wheels of the carriage first rise with a great effort on top of a log, and then plunge into fathomless depths of mud! Rather than such jolting, it is better that the experimental speeches should never rise above the level of mere talk, and thus maintain a uniform progress. In due time all qualified persons can lift their extemporaneous words as high as the utmost reach of the pen. But first must be gained the power of standing unprotected by a paper wall, face to face with an audience and employing every faculty as calmly and efficiently as in the study. Practice in talking to the people will make this possible and easy, but nothing else will.

CHAPTER V

UTILITY OF DEBATING SOCIETIES

Comparatively little attention is paid to the direct cultivation of extemporaneous oratory in schools and colleges. Indirectly, much help is given by teaching many things which go to furnish the orator with ideas and words, but the combination of these into that noble effort of human genius—a speech—is left to individual research or to accident. A few schools of oratory have been founded which give a large and probably disproportionate share of attention to elocution in the form of stage or dramatic reading; but even the best of these are as yet but entering upon their real work of cultivating thoroughly the power of persuasive public speech. When each college shall have a chair of extempore speech, and each academy shall give as much attention to unpremeditated utterances in conversation and public address as is now bestowed upon Greek or Latin, the oratory of pulpit, bar, platform, and legislature will be of a vastly higher type.

Some newspaper critics have deprecated teaching the art of speech on the ground that there is already too much public talking. This view, if seriously entertained, is very narrow and misleading. Not more, but better speech—an increase of quality, rather than quantity—would result from cultivation, and improved methods. And it may also be argued that if a great part of the work of life is found in convincing, instructing, and persuading our fellows, an abundance of speech is absolutely required. As freedom and mental activity increase, the only practicable modes of leading and governing men, which rest upon persuasive speech, will be more urgently demanded. In a state where the will of one man is law, political speech has little place; and in a Church where independent thought is heresy and the mass of the people accept unquestioningly the precise form of faith in which they were born, preaching will have a very narrow field. But in our own country it is our boast that we determine every subject by free discussion; and it is clear that a man who can take no part in the oral battles that are continually waged about him is placed at a great disadvantage.

But the literary societies generally connected with schools do afford very valuable help in acquiring the art of oratory. Not only their formal exercises, but their discussion of points of order and procedure, and the management of the business and government of such societies, call out talking talent. Debating societies or lyceums give the same kind of facilities to speakers outside of educational halls. A spirited debate on some topic not above the comprehension of the debaters affords one of the best possible means of acquiring the prime faculties of assurance and fluency. In such debates the question is chosen, the sides assigned, and ample time given for that kind of preparation which can only be effectually made in the general study of the subject. There is no great temptation to write a speech for a coming debate, as its formal sentences would fit poorly into the line of argument, the course of which cannot be foreseen, even if their substance should not be anticipated by a speaker on the same side. But the more general knowledge of the subject in its entire range that can be acquired the better, so long as it does not overwhelm the speaker. The opening speech may indeed be planned in advance with some definiteness, but all others will be colored and modified by the situation into which the debate has been drawn. Each participant is under a strong stimulus to do his best, sure, if successful, of warm approval by his colleagues and sweet triumph over his opponents. After the opening speech each contestant will have the time his predecessor is speaking for arranging arguments and preparing an answer. The stimulus of contradiction rouses every faculty to the highest energy. Each argument is scrutinized for the purpose of discovering its weak point, and nothing will pass on trust. It may as well be acknowledged that the gladiatorial spirit, though in a modified form, is still rife in the civilized world. The "joy of conflict" may be tasted as well in the sharp encounters of an earnest debate upon some topic of absorbing interest as on the battle-field. A society which furnishes its members continual opportunity for speech, under such conditions cannot fail to be a powerful educator in the direction of extemporaneous speech. In such encounters, the freedom that belongs to this kind of address is most highly appreciated, and the mistaken considerations of dignity and propriety which so often take all life and heart from speech can have little weight. Debates have indeed been occasionally carried on by means of essays in place of speeches, but such encounters have been tame and listless affairs, and have soon given place to the real article. Among the American statesmen who have taken their first lessons in the art which paved their way to greatness in country debating societies may be reckoned Henry Clay, Abraham Lincoln, James A. Garfield, and many others only less eminent.

Enough inducements, we trust, have been set forth to lead every student of speech to find or make an opportunity for availing himself of this capital means of cultivation. Let him enter upon the work of debating, earnestly resolving (after the first few efforts) to do the very best in his power. Let him arrange his material carefully, select a striking mode of opening each address, and strive to close in such a manner as to leave the best effect on the minds of his hearers. As he debates for improvement rather than for immediate victory, he will, of course, despise all tricks and seek to win fairly, or—what is just as important a lesson—he will learn to accept defeat gracefully.

The skeletons of two speeches on opposite sides of the same question are here presented for the purpose of showing how a simple plan will hold to the proper place all the thoughts and arguments that may be accumulated.

The same form of outline is used as in the preceding chapter.

Question

Would the annexation of Cuba to the United States be beneficial?

Affirmative Argument.

Introduction.—How small and hemmed in by powerful countries the United States would have been if no annexations had ever been made. To annex Cuba would be no new policy.

Discussion. Argument First.—Favorable location of Cuba and commercial value to the United States.

Argument Second.—The great riches and beauty of the Island, which make it very desirable.

Argument Third.—Advantages to the people of Cuba themselves, in belonging to a great and free nation.

Conclusion.—All previous annexations had to encounter strong opposition when first proposed, but are now acknowledged to have been good policy. So, if Cuba is brought under our flag, opposition will die out and all parties be glad of the result.

Negative Argument

Introduction.—Plausible but inconclusive nature of the argument advanced on the other side. Previous annexations may not have been good, though opposition ceased when it could avail nothing. Even if all former annexations were beneficial this might not be, as all attending circumstances are so widely different.

Discussion. Argument First.—The nation has already as much territory as can be well governed. An increase would lead to grave dangers.

Argument Second.—The people of Cuba are different in language, race, and religion from the majority of the people of the United States; have different customs, and are unacquainted with the working of our institutions. They could not therefore be transformed easily into good citizens.

Conclusion.—Dreadful wars and calamities have arisen in all ages and all parts of the world from greediness in absorbing territory—"earth hunger," as the Germans call it. To annex Cuba would involve present and future danger.

CHAPTER VI

THOUGHT AND EMOTION

Two kinds of preparation contribute to the production of eloquence. One is the preparation of the speaker, the other of the speech. The first is fully as important as the second. In ordinary cases both are indispensable. Some "born orators" speak well without appearing to pay any attention to the improvement of their faculties. Others are occasionally eloquent on a topic without special preparation. Yet these cases when closely examined will be found apparent rather than real exceptions to the rule above stated. The man who seems never to have cultivated the power of speech, and is yet able to blaze into fervid eloquence at will, has usually concealed his preparation or carried it on in such uncommon methods that they have not been recognized as preparations. On the other hand, a man who speaks well without a moment's warning can do so only when the subject is thoroughly familiar to him. A ready and self-possessed speaker may grasp thoughts which have been long maturing in his mind, and give them forth to an audience in obedience to an unexpected summons, but if he is called upon when he knows nothing whatever of his subject, failure is inevitable, though he may possibly veil it more or less in a stream of platitudes. Ask a man at a moment's warning to give an astronomical lecture. If he is perfectly familiar with the subject in general, and is also a practical orator, he may succeed well without preparing a special speech. But if he is ignorant of Astronomy, what kind of an address can he make? If he is the most eloquent man in the nation that faculty will avail him nothing, for he cannot extemporize the names of the planets, the laws which govern their motions, or any of the facts out of which his lecture must be woven. Precisely the same necessity of adequate information exists in every other field of intelligence. The ignorant man cannot possibly tell that which he does not know, although he may make a great show of knowledge out of small material; but even to do that with certainty requires careful premeditation and arrangement.

In this and following chapters we wish to treat of the kind of cultivation which makes a man ready to speak. The field is here very wide and some general considerations must be introduced, but we hope also to give valuable practical directions, especially to those who are yet at the beginning of their career.

In considering man as a speaker, we may classify his faculties into two broad divisions; those which furnish the *materials* of communication with his fellows; and those which furnish the *means* of such communication. The first class gives rise to thoughts and emotions in man's own breast; the second enables him to arouse similar thoughts and emotions in the breasts of others. Our course, therefore, will be to consider, first, thought and emotion, and afterward those powers of body and mind by which we express, that is, press out from ourselves toward the receptive faculties of our fellow beings.

Thought, in the broad sense here given, embraces the knowledge of all facts, and all the reasoning that may be based upon those facts. *Emotion* is the mental feeling or response to knowledge, and comprises love, hate, joy, fear, sorrow, and hope. These two elements are the broad basis of all eloquence. Keen, profound, far-reaching thought—in other words, thought raised to its highest terms—and quick, sensitive, powerful emotion, are necessary to the highest eloquence. Compared with them, mere verbal fluency is less than dust in the balance. But such a combination—the highest degree of both thought and emotion—is rare, and many degrees less than the highest of either is available for genuine eloquence. To increase either or both, if it can be done without any corresponding sacrifice, is to increase eloquence in precisely the same proportion.

Education in the popular sense is the cultivation of thought with the added faculty of language. But we prefer to consider the latter power separately as one among the means of communicating thought.

How, then, shall thought-power be increased? There is no royal road. Every one of the faculties by which knowledge is accumulated and arranged or digested into new forms grows stronger by being employed upon its own appropriate objects. Exercise is then the means by which the material of knowledge is gathered, and all faculties strengthened for future gathering. Each fact gained adds to the treasury of thought. A broad and liberal education is of exceeding advantage. This may or may not be of the schools. Indeed, they too often substitute a knowledge of words for a knowledge of things. That fault is very serious to the orator, for the only way by which even language can be effectively taught, is by giving terms to objects, the nature of which has been previously learned.

But many persons need to speak who cannot obtain an education in the usual sense of the words—that is, college or seminary training. Must they keep their lips forever closed on that account? By no means.

A thousand examples, some of them the most eminent speakers the world has produced, encourage them to hope. Let such persons learn all they can. Wide, well-selected, and systematic reading will do wonders in supplying the necessary thought-material. Every book of history, biography, travels, popular science, which is carefully read, and its contents fixed in the mind, will be available for the purposes of oratory. Here a word of advice may be offered, which, if heeded, will be worth many months of technical education at the best colleges in the land; it is this: have always at hand some work that in its own sphere possesses real and permanent merit, and read it daily until completed. If notes are made of its contents, and the book itself kept on hand for reference, so much the better. If some friend can be found who will hear you relate in your own words what you have read, this also will be of great value. Many persons, especially in our own country, spend time enough in reading the minute details of the daily papers to make them thoroughly acquainted in ten years with forty volumes of the most useful books in the world. Think of it! This number may include nearly all the literary masterpieces. Which mode of spending the time will produce the best results? One newspaper read daily would amount to more than three hundred in a year, and allowing each paper to be equal to ten ordinary book pages, the result would be three thousand pages annually, or six volumes of five hundred pages each. In ten years this would reach *sixty* volumes! This number, comprising the world's best books in history, poetry, science, and general literature, might be read slowly, with meditation and diligent note-taking, by the most busy man who was willing to employ his leisure in that way. Libraries and books are now brought within the reach of all, and the mass of what man knows can be learned in outline by any student who thirsts for knowledge. While thus engaged the student is on the direct road toward oratorical efficiency, though such knowledge will not in itself constitute eloquence. It is but one of its elements. Neither will the speaker have to wait until any definite quantity of reading has been accomplished before it becomes serviceable to him. All that he learns will be immediately available, and, with proper effort, the facility of speech and the material for speaking will keep pace with each other.

But personal observation of life and nature are just as necessary as reading. The world of books is very extensive, but it yields its treasures only to persons who bring to its study some independent knowledge of their own. We cannot hope to add much to the world's stock of knowledge by what we see with our own eyes, but what we do see and hear will interpret for us what we learn from the far wider world of books. Gibbon tells us that his militia service, though of no great advantage in itself, was afterward very useful to the historian of the Roman Empire. What we behold of the landscape around us lays the foundation for understanding what poets and travelers tell us of other landscapes we may never see. Book knowledge will become real and vivid just in proportion as it is brought into comparison with the observation of our own senses. To the orator, this is far more important than to the ordinary student, for it adds greatly to the royal faculty of imagination. A description from the lips of a speaker who beholds at the moment a mental picture, accurate as a photograph, and bright with color, will be very different from another description built up only of words, however well chosen and melodious the latter may be. A little dabbling in natural science, a few experiments tried, an occasional peep through telescope or microscope at the worlds they open, and all other means of bringing knowledge under the scrutiny of our own senses, will greatly contribute to the power of the orator.

The reasoning faculties must also be trained by exercise upon their own objects. The knowledge which has been gathered from personal observation or from the testimony of others in books will furnish material, but will not enable us to reason. Logic and mathematics have considerable utility as guides, but they cannot supply the want of continuous application of the processes of argument and deduction. No man becomes a reasoner from merely learning the mode in which the reason operates. Of two persons, one of whom understands every mood of the syllogism and the source of every fallacy, while the other has no technical knowledge of logic, but has been engaged in careful reasoning, discussion, and argument, all his life, it may easily happen that the latter will be the better reasoner of the two—just as a man might learn from the books all the rules of the game of croquet, and yet be beaten by another who continually handled the mallet, but had never read a single rule. Practice makes perfect. Essay writing, constructing arguments, tracing effects back to their causes, making careful comparison of all things that can be compared, in short, bringing our judgment to bear upon all facts, forming our own opinions of every event, and being always ready to give a reason to those who ask,—these modes of exercise will make the faculty of reason grow continually stronger. It is not pretended that these or any other modes of cultivation can make all minds equal, but they will improve any one—the lowest as surely as the most active—though the interval after both have been thus exercised will remain as great as before.

Extempore speech itself, when practiced upon carefully arranged plans or models as recommended hereafter, is one of the most powerful modes of cultivating the logical faculty. To construct plans, so that all thoughts accumulated upon a given subject may be unfolded in a natural and orderly manner, cannot fail to exercise the reasoning faculties, and impart corresponding strength to them.

But how shall emotion be cultivated? The wisest speech, if deep feeling neither throbs in the words nor is manifested in delivery, cannot be eloquent. The orator can only speak forth from an aroused and excited nature. There is a kind of intellectual excitation kindled by the presentation of truth which is sufficiently effective when instruction is the only object. But to persuade and move men—the usual aim of the orator—requires passion. No pretense will avail the extempore speaker. He will infallibly be detected if counterfeiting, and to succeed in exhibiting feeling he must really feel. There are but two things which can arouse feeling—care for a cause or for persons. Many a man is eloquent when "riding his hobby," though at no other time. He has thought so much upon that special subject, and has so thoroughly identified himself with it, that everything relating to it becomes invested with personal interest. Any cause which can thus be made personal will be apt to arouse feeling. It would be wise, therefore, for an orator to identify himself as closely as possible with all manner of good causes which come within his reach. Then such well-springs of emotion will gush out easily and frequently.

This mode of excitation is largely intellectual in its character. The next to be described has more to do with the affections. The clergyman wants to secure the welfare of his congregation, and the better he is acquainted with them individually the stronger will be this wish. The lawyer is but a poor attorney if he does not so identify himself with his client as to feel more than a professional interest in the latter's success. The politician needs no exhortation to rouse his enthusiasm for his party and his chief. All these are instances of that care for persons which adds so greatly to the powers of effective speech. The plain inference, therefore, is that the speaker will gain largely by identifying himself as closely as possible with the interests of men, and by cultivating love for them. A cynical or indifferent spirit makes a fearful discount from the possibilities of eloquence. Only the greatest qualities in other directions can prevent it from proving fatal.

The power and sensitiveness of emotions founded upon intimate knowledge and partnership of interest go far to explain the wonderful eloquence of the old Greeks. Their country was the native land of eloquence. This arose not so much from the character of that gifted race as from the fact that each speaker personally knew his audience and had an intimate, material interest in the affairs he discussed. They regarded their opponents as terribly bad men. Their own lives and the lives of many of their friends were not unfrequently involved in the questions they discussed. The States were so small, and the personal element so important, that strongly aroused feeling became inevitable. The discussion of war or peace before an audience who knew that if they voted war their town might be besieged by the enemy within a fortnight, was sure to be eagerly listened to. No platitudes would be tolerated. The orators spoke before their neighbors, some of them friendly, others bitter enemies who were seeking in each word they uttered an occasion for their ruin. Much of the wonderful power of Demosthenes arose from the deep solicitude felt by himself and excited in his hearers as they watched the swiftly coming ruin of their common country.

It is also a law of human nature that we feel deeply for that which has cost us great labor. The collector of old china or of entomological specimens learns to greatly value the ugly dishes and bugs he gathers, though others may despise them. The more of real work we do in the world, the deeper the hold our hearts take upon it. This is one of the secrets of the power of goodness as an element of oratory. It was long ago declared that a good man, other things being equal, will be a better speaker than a bad man. His affections are called forth by a greater variety of objects. Yet hate can make a man eloquent as well as love, and some of the most eloquent orations ever uttered partook largely of this baleful inspiration. But the occasions on which noble feelings may rise into eloquence are far more numerous and important.

Why should not a man train himself to take a deep interest in all that is brought familiarly to his notice? This wide range of sympathy is one of the marks which distinguishes a great from a small mind. It has been said that "lunar politics" can have no possible interests for the inhabitants of this globe. But who can be sure of this, if there be such a thing as "lunar politics"? The wider our knowledge the more we recognize the possibility of interests which we had not before dreamed of. If there are inhabitants on the moon, and if we have an immortal existence, it is far from impossible that we might some time be brought into the closest connection with them. No man can tell the bearing of a new fact upon human welfare, more than he can write the history of a new-born babe. At any rate, every fact is a part of the great system of truth which lies all about us, and which is adapted to the needs of our intellect. Let it also be remembered that all men are kindred, and that we should make common cause with them. When this comes to be the habitual attitude of the mind, not as a mere sentiment, but as a strong and steady impulse, impassioned speech on any great theme affecting the interests of nations or individual men will be easy.

Emotion cannot be feigned, neither can it be directly roused by an effort of the will. We cannot say, "Now I will be in a furious passion," or, "Now I will be inflamed with wrath against this great wrong," for the mere sake of speaking better upon the subject in hand. But we can gaze upon a great wrong, and meditate upon the evil it involves, until the tides of indignant emotion arise in our breast. Many a well-prepared speech has failed of effect, because the orator was so anxious about the form of his address and his own popularity as to lose interest in the subject itself. Sometimes speeches read or recited fail from an opposite cause. The interest has once been aroused, and having burned during the protracted period of composition, it cools and cannot be recalled. No energy, declamation, or elegance of diction can redeem this capital defect.

To tell a man in general terms how he may widen his sympathies and enter into the closest bonds with his fellows is difficult. It is much easier to tell him what not to do. The hermits of the desert took exactly the wrong course. They lost the power of eloquence except upon some theme which could be wedded to their solitary musings. Peter the Hermit was roused to fury by the tales of wrongs to pilgrims in the Holy City—almost the only thing that could have made him eloquent. But on that one topic he spoke like a man inspired and was able to call all Europe to arms. Whatever separates from the common interests of humanity must diminish the power or at least the range of genuine emotion. To know a great many men, to understand their business affairs, to enter into their joy and fear, to watch the feelings that rise and fall in their hearts, is sure to deepen our own feelings by unconscious imitation and sympathy. Each new friend is an added power of noblest emotion—a new point at which the world takes hold of our hearts. How many persons are eloquent for a cause only! On the other hand, some men care nothing for general principles, but will throw their whole soul into a conflict for friends.

That man is well furnished for eloquence who knows a great deal, who can mentally combine, arrange, and reason correctly upon what he knows, who feels a personal interest in every fact with which his memory is stored, and every principle which can be deduced from those facts, and who has so great an interest in his fellows that all deeds which affect them awaken the same response in his heart as if done to himself. He will then possess all the necessary treasures of thought, and will himself be warmed by the fires of emotion. The only remaining problem will be to find the manner of communicating his thought and emotion in undiminished force to others through the medium of speech.

The mode of cultivating the powers necessary to this end will next engage our attention.

CHAPTER VII

Language

The preceding chapter dealt with those faculties which provide the materials of speech, and in one sense was scarcely appropriate to a treatise designed to show the best modes of communicating knowledge. Yet it was difficult to approach the subject intelligibly in any other way. So much has been said about the natural power of oratory that it was necessary to define its character and to show how it might be supplemented by cultivation. But it is more directly our task to point out the mode of improving the communicative faculties.

First in importance among these stands language. Without its assistance thought could not be consecutively imparted. Some vague and intangible conceptions might arise within our own minds, but even these could not be given to other minds without the medium of words. The power of language is distinct from general intellectual ability. It by no means follows that a man who possesses important thoughts and deep emotions will be able to communicate them well; but a very moderate endowment of the word-faculty may be so cultivated as to fulfill every requirement. Diligent practice in the methods advised below will enable the great majority of men to express their thoughts with fullness and accuracy.

There are certain laws in every language made binding by custom, which cannot be transgressed without exposing the offender to the severe penalty of ridicule and contempt. These laws form the basis of grammar, and must be thoroughly learned. If a man has been under the influence of good models from childhood, correctness will be a matter almost of instinct; but the reverse of this is frequently the case. Even then there is but little difficulty experienced by any one who will take the necessary pains, in learning to write in accordance with the rules of speech, and when this power has been attained there is a standard formed by which to judge our spoken words. But it is not enough for the extempore speaker to be able to reduce his sentences to correctness by recasting, pruning, or adding to them. They should be required to present themselves at first in correct form and in rounded completeness. He has no time to think of right or wrong constructions, and the only safe way, therefore, is to make the right so habitual that the wrong will not once be thought of. In other words, we must not only be able to express ourselves correctly by tongue and pen, but the very current of unspoken words that flows in our brains must be shaped in full conformity to the laws of language. When we exercise the power of continuous grammatical thinking, there will be no difficulty in avoiding the ridiculous blunders which are supposed to be inseparable from extempore speech.

Correctness in pronunciation is also of importance. Usage has given each word its authorized sound, which no person can frequently mistake without rendering himself liable to the easiest and most damaging of all criticisms. Bad pronunciation produces another and extremely hurtful effect upon extempore speech. The mental effort necessary to discriminate between two modes of pronouncing a word, neither of which is known to be right, diverts the mind from the subject and produces embarrassment and hesitation. Accuracy in the use of words, which is a charm in spoken no less than written language, may also be impaired from the same cause; for if two terms that may be used for the same idea are thought of, only one of which can be pronounced with certainty, that one will be preferred, even if the other be the more suitable. The extemporizer ought to be so familiar with the sound of all common words that none but the right pronunciation and accent will ever enter his mind.

Fluency and accuracy in the use of words are two qualities that have often been confounded, though perfectly distinct. To the speaker they are of equal importance, while the writer has far more need of the latter. All words have their own peculiar shades of meaning. They have been builded up into their present shape through long ages. By strange turns and with many a curious history have they glided into the significations they now bear; and each one is imbedded in the minds of the people as the representative of certain definite ideas. Words are delicate paints that, to the untutored eye, may seem of one color, but each has its own place in the picture painted by the hand of genius, and can be supplanted by no other. Many methods have been suggested for learning these fine shades of meaning. The study of Greek and Latin has been urged as the best and almost the only way: such study may be very useful for discipline, and will give much elementary knowledge of the laws of language: but the man who knows no other tongue than his own need not consider himself debarred from the very highest place as a master of words. The careful study of a good etymological dictionary will, in time, give him about all the valuable information bearing upon this subject that he could obtain from the study of many languages. In general reading, let him mark every word he does not perfectly understand, and from the dictionary find its origin, the meaning of its roots, and its varied significations at the present day. This will make the word as familiar as an old acquaintance, and when he meets it again he will notice if the author uses it correctly. The student may not be able to examine every word in the language, but by this mode he will be led to think of the meaning of each one he sees; and from this silent practice he will learn the beauty and power of English as fully as if he sought it through the literatures of Greece and Rome. If this habit is long continued it will cause words to be used correctly in thinking as well as in speaking. To read a dictionary consecutively and carefully (ignoring the old story about its frequent change of subject) will also be found very profitable.

Translating from any language, ancient or modern, will have just the same tendency to teach accurate expression as careful original composition. In either case the improvement comes from the search for words that exactly convey certain ideas, and it matters not what the source of the ideas may be. The use of a good thesaurus, or storehouse of words, may also be serviceable by showing in one view all the words that relate to any subject.

But none of these methods will greatly increase fluency. There is a practical difference between merely knowing a term and that easy use of it which only habit can give. Elihu Burritt, with his knowledge of fifty languages, has often been surpassed in fluency, force, and variety of expression by an unlettered farmer, because the few words the latter knew were always ready. There is no way to increase this easy and fluent use of language without much practice in utterance. Where and how can such practice be obtained?

Conversation affords an excellent means for this kind of improvement. We do not mean the running fire of question and answer, glancing so rapidly back and forth as to allow no time for premeditating or explaining anything, but real and rational talk—an exchange of thoughts and ideas clearly and intelligibly expressed. The man who engages much in this kind of conversation can scarcely fail to become an adept in the art of expressing his thoughts in appropriate language. Talk much; express your ideas in the best manner possible; if difficult at first, persevere, and it will become easier. Thus you will learn eloquence in the best and most pleasing school. The common conversational style—that in which man deals directly with his fellow man—is the germ of true oratory. It may be amplified and systematized; but talking bears to eloquence the same relation that the soil does to the tree that springs out of its bosom.

But the best thoughts of men and the noblest expressions are seldom found floating on the sea of common talk. To drink the deepest inspiration, our minds must often come in loving communion with the wise and mighty of all ages. In the masterpieces of literature we will find "thought knit close to thought," and, what is still more to our present purpose, words so applied as to breathe and live. These passages should be read until their spirit sinks into our hearts and their melody rings like a blissful song in our ears. To memorize many such passages will be a profitable employment. The words of which such masterpieces are composed, with the meanings they bear in their several places, will thus be fixed in our minds ready to drop on our tongues when needed. This conning of beautiful passages is not now recommended for the purpose of quotation, although they may often be used in that manner to good advantage, but simply to print the individual words with their signification more deeply in memory.

This may be effected, also, by memorizing selections from our own best writings. What is thus used should be highly polished, and yet preserve, as far as possible, the natural form of expression. Carried to a moderate extent, this exercise tends to elevate the character of our extemporaneous efforts by erecting a standard that is our own, and therefore suited to our tastes and capacities; but if made habitual, it will induce a reliance upon the memory rather than on the power of spontaneous production, and thus destroy the faculty it was designed to cultivate.

But no means of cultivating fluency in language can rival extempore speech itself. The only difficulty is to find a sufficient number of occasions to speak. Long intervals of preparation have great advantages as far as the gathering of material for discourse is concerned; but they have disadvantages, also, which can only be overcome by more diligent effort in other directions.

Clear and definite ideas greatly increase the power of language. When a thought is fully understood it falls into words as naturally as a summer cloud, riven by the lightning, dissolves into rain. So easy is it to express a series of ideas, completely mastered, that a successful speaker once said, "It is a man's own fault if he ever fails. Let him prepare as he ought, and there is no danger." The assertion was too strong, for failure may come from other causes than a want of preparation. Yet the continuance of careful drill, in connection with frequent speaking and close preparation, will give very great ease and certainty of expression. The "blind but eloquent" preacher, Milburn, says that he gave four years of his life—the time spent as chaplain at Washington—to acquire the power of speaking correctly and easily without the previous use of the pen, and he declares that he considers the time well spent. His style is diffuse, sparkling, rhetorical, the most difficult to acquire, though not by any means the most valuable. An earnest, nervous, and yet elegant style may be formed by those who have the necessary qualifications in much shorter time.

CHAPTER VIII

IMAGINATION

Nothing adds more to the brilliancy and effectiveness of oratory than the royal faculty of imagination. This weird and glorious power deals with truth as well as fiction and gives to its fortunate possessor the creative, life-breathing spirit of poetry.

Listen to the description of natural scenery by a person of imagination, and afterward by another destitute of that faculty! Each may be perfectly accurate and refer to the same objects, even enumerating the same particulars in the same order; but the one gives a catalogue, the other a picture. In relating a story or enforcing an argument, the same difference in the vividness of impression is apparent.

It is said of Henry Ward Beecher, who possesses a strong imagination, that the people would listen with delighted attention if he only described the mode in which a potato grew! He would see a thousand beauties in its budding and blossoming, and paint the picture so vividly as to command universal attention.

The Bible, which is the most popular of all books, is pre-eminently a book of imagination. Nowhere is loftier or more beautiful imagery employed, or wrought into more exquisite forms. A few short and simple words paint pictures that the world looks upon with astonishment from age to age. Paradise Lost, the most sublime imaginative poem in the language of man, drew much of its inspiration from a few passages in Genesis. Job and Isaiah are without rivals in the power of picturing by means of words, sublime objects beyond the grasp of mortal vision.

While illustrations and comparisons flow principally from the reasoning faculties, their beauty and sparkle come from imagination. Without its influence these may explain and simplify, but they have no power to interest the hearer or elevate the tenor of discourse.

How may imagination be cultivated? It is said that "Poets are born, not made," but the foundation of every other faculty also is in nature, while all are useless, unless improved, and applied. Imagination will increase in vigor and activity by proper use. Its function is to form complete mental images from the detached materials furnished by the senses. It gathers from all sources and mixes and mingles until a picture is produced. The proper way to cultivate it lies in forming abundance of just such pictures and in finishing them with all possible care. Let the orator, on the canvas of the mind, paint in full size and perfect coloring, every part of his speech which relates to material or visible things. Illustrations also can usually be represented in picturesque form. We do not now speak of outward representation, but of viewing all objects in clear distinctness, through the eye of the mind. It is not enough for the speaker, if he would reach the highest success, to gather all the facts he wishes to use, to arrange them in the best order, or even to premeditate the very form of words. Instead of the latter process, he may more profitably strive to embrace all that can be pictured in one mental view. If he can summon before him in the moment of description the very scenes and events about which he is discoursing, and behold them vividly as in a waking dream, it is probable that his auditors will see them in the same manner. A large part of all discourses may thus be made pictorial. In Ivanhoe, one of the characters looks out through a castle window and describes to a wounded knight within the events of the assault which was being made upon the castle. Any person could describe the most stirring scene vividly and well in the moment of witnessing it. A strong imagination enables a speaker or poet to see those things he speaks of almost as accurately and impressively as if passing before his bodily eyes, and often with far more brightness of color. To make the effort to see what we write or read will have a powerful effect in improving the imaginative faculty.

Reading and carefully pondering the works of those who have imagination in high degree will also be helpful. The time devoted to the enjoyment of great poems is not lost to the orator. They give richness and tone to his mind, introduce him into scenes of ideal beauty, and furnish him with many a striking thought and glowing image.

Most of the sciences give as full scope to imagination in its best workings as poetry itself. Astronomy and geology are pre-eminent in this particular. Everything about them is grand. They deal with immense periods of time, vast magnitudes, and sublime histories. Each science requires the formation of mental images and thus gives the advantages we have already pointed out. It is possible for a scientific man to deal exclusively with the shell rather than the substance of science, with its technical names and definitions rather than its grand truths; but in this case the fault is with himself rather than with his subject. The dryness of scientific and even mathematical studies relates only to the preliminary departments. A philosopher once said that success in science and in poetry depended upon the same faculties. He was very nearly right. The poet is a creator who forms new worlds of his own. The greatest of their number thus describes the process by which imagination performs its magic.

"The poet's eye, in a fine frenzy rolling,
Doth glance from heaven to earth, from earth to heaven;
And, as imagination bodies forth
The forms of things unknown, the poet's pen
Turns them to shapes and gives to airy nothing
A local habitation and a name.
Such tricks hath strong imagination."

Almost the same result must be reached in many departments of science, with the aid of only a few scattered facts for a basis. The geologist has some broken bones, withered leaves, and fragments of rock, from which to reconstruct the primitive world. From the half-dozen facts observed through his telescope, the astronomer pictures the physical condition of distant planets. In every science the same need exists for imagination in its highest, most truthful function, and the same opportunity is, therefore, afforded for its cultivation.

An eminent elocutionist frequently urged his classes to employ all pauses in mentally picturing the idea contained in the coming sentence. He declared that by this means the expression of the voice was rendered more rich and true. In uttering our own words this process is at once more easy and more fruitful in varied advantages.

CHAPTER IX

Voice and Gesture

Voice and gesture form the immediate link between the speaker and his audience. The value of good quality in both is sometimes over-estimated, though it is always considerable. A good voice, well managed, gives powerful and vivid expression to thought, but cannot supply the absence of it. Neither is such a voice indispensable. Many instances of high success against vocal disadvantages might be mentioned; but these only prove that other excellencies may atone for a single defect. We can never be indifferent to the charms of a good voice, that modulates with every emotion and responds to the finest shades of feeling. It has much of the pleasing quality of music.

But this harmony cannot be evoked by merely mechanical training. To teach the pupil just what note on the musical scale he must strike to express a particular emotion, how much of an inflection must be used to express joy or sorrow, and how many notes down the scale mark a complete suspension of sense, is absurd: speech can never be set to music.

But let it not be inferred from this that voice cultivation is useless. The more perfect the instrument for the expression of thought can be made, the better it will be fitted for its high office. An orator may profitably spend a little time daily for years in training the voice, for it is a faculty he must continually employ, and none is more susceptible of improvement. The passion evoked in animated speech will demand for its adequate expression almost every note and key within the compass of the voice; and unless it has previously been trained into strength on each of these, it will fail or grow weary. The proper kind of preparation operates by exploring the range of the voice, testing its capabilities, and improving each tone. This work is not imitative or slavish. It is only like putting an instrument in tune before beginning a musical performance.

To give full elocutionary instruction here would be aside from our purpose; but a few useful modes of practice may be pointed out.

Good articulation is of prime importance. Nothing will contribute more to secure this valuable quality than the separation of words into their elements of sound and continued practice on each element as thus isolated. Phonetic shorthand affords a good means for making such analysis, or the same purpose may be accomplished by means of the marks of pronunciation found in any dictionary. As we practice these elements of sound we will discover the exact nature of any defect of articulation we may suffer from, and can drill upon the sounds that are difficult until they become easy. When we have thus learned to pronounce these few elements—not much above forty in number—and can follow them into all their combinations, we have mastered the alphabet of utterance. It will also contribute greatly to strengthen the voice and make it pliable, if we continue the same practice on these elements at different degrees of elevation on the musical scale until we can utter each one in full, round distinctness, at any pitch from the deepest bass to the shrillest note ever used in speech. This will bring all varieties of modulation within easy reach.

Practice on these elements is also a very effective mode of strengthening weak voices. By pronouncing them one by one, with gradually increasing force, the degree of loudness we can attain at any pitch, will be greatly extended. The amount of improvement that may be made would be incredible if it were not so often exemplified. Every teacher of elocution can testify of students, the power of whose voices has thus been multiplied many fold; and almost equal advantages may be reaped in persevering private practice.

Following on the same line, we may learn to enunciate the elements, and especially the short vowels, in a quick, sharp tone, more rapidly than the ticking of a watch, and with the clearness of a bell. This will enable the speaker to avoid drawling, and be very fast when desirable, without falling into indistinctness. Then, by an opposite process, other sounds, especially the long vowels, may be prolonged with every degree of force from the faintest to the fullest. Perseverance in these two exercises will so improve the voice that no hall will be too large for its compass.

The differing extension of sounds, as well as their pitch and variations in force, constitute the *perspective* of speech and give it an agreeable variety, like the mingling of light and shade in a well-executed picture. The opposite of this, a dull, dead uniformity, with each word uttered in the same key, with the same force, and at the same degree of speed, becomes well-nigh unbearable; while perpetual modulation, reflecting in each rise and fall, each storm and calm of sound, the living thought within, is the perfection of nature, which the best art can only copy.

All vocal exercises are of an essentially preparatory character. In the moment of speech details may safely be left to the impulse of nature. Supply the capability by previous discipline, and then allow passion to clothe itself in the most natural forms. There is such a vital connection between emotion and the tones of voice, that emphasis and inflection will be as spontaneous, on the part of the disciplined speaker, as breathing. Rules remembered in the act of speaking tend to destroy all life and freshness of utterance.

When bad habits have been corrected, the voice made supple and strong, confidence attained, and deep feeling evoked in the speaker's breast, there will be little need to care for the minutiæ of elocution. The child that is burnt needs no instruction in the mode of crying out. Let nature have her way, untrammeled by art, and all feelings will dominate the voice and cause every hearer to recognize their nature and participate in them. In this way we may not attain the brilliancy of theatric clap-trap, but we will be able to give "the touch of nature that makes the whole world kin."

If carefully guarded, the faculty of imitation may be of great service in the management of the voice. The sounds that express sympathy and passion are heard everywhere, forming a medium of communication more subtle and widespread than any language of earth. From the example of great orators we may learn what true excellence is, and become able to reproduce some, at least, of their effects. It would be hurtful to confine our attention too long to one model, for true excellence is many-sided, and if we continually view only one of its phases we are apt to fall into slavish imitation—one of the greatest of all vices. By having many examples to look upon, and using them only to elevate our own ideal, we will escape this danger. The models before us will urge us to greater exertions and the whole level of our attainments be raised.

There are abundant faults to mar the freedom and naturalness of delivery, and the speaker who would be truly natural must watch diligently for them and exterminate them without mercy. The sing-song tone, the scream, the lisp, the guttural and tremulous tones, the rhythmical emphasis which falls like a trip-hammer at measured intervals, are specimens of common, bad habits that should be weeded out as fast as they push through the soil; and if the speaker's egotism is too great to see them, or his taste not pure enough, some friend should point them out. Even the advice of an enemy conveyed in the unpleasant form of sarcasm and ridicule may be profitably used for the purpose of reform and improvement.

Should a conversational tone be employed in speaking? This question has often been asked, and much difference of opinion evoked, but it may be satisfactorily answered. The language of conversation is the language of nature in its most unfettered form, and it should, therefore, be the basis of all speech. The same variety and character of intonations used in it should be employed in every variety of oratory. But conversation itself varies widely with varying circumstances. The man talking with a friend across a river will speak less rapidly but more loudly than if he held that friend by the hand. In speaking to a number at once, the orator must, in order to be heard, speak more forcibly and distinctly than in addressing one only. With this explanation, it may be laid down as a safe rule that a speech should begin in a conversational manner. But should it continue in the same way? A deep, full tone—the orotund of the elocutionist—will make a stronger impression than a shrill, feeble utterance. And as conversation becomes earnest even between two persons, there is the tendency to stronger and more impressive tones. This same tendency will be a sufficient guide in speech. A trained man giving utterance to a well-prepared speech, upon a theme which appeals to his own emotions, will adopt those oratorical tones which form a proper medium for eloquence, without a single thought given to that subject during the moment of delivery. Begin as a man who is talking to a number of his friends upon an interesting subject; then, as the interest deepens, let go all restraint. As passion rises like an inflowing tide, the voice will be so fully possessed by it and so filled out and strengthened as to produce all the effect of which its compass is capable. It will deepen into the thunder roll when that is needed, and at the right time will grow soft and pathetic.

But above almost every other error that the speaker can commit, beware of thinking that you must be loud in order to be impressive. Nothing is more disgusting than that interminable roar, beginning with a shout, and continuing to split the speaker's throat and the hearer's ears all through the discourse. This fault is not uncommon in the pulpit, especially among those who desire a reputation for extraordinary fervor and earnestness. But it is the worst kind of monotony. The loudness of tone, that applied at the right place would be overpowering, loses all power except to disgust and weary an audience. It expresses no more thought or sentiment than the lashing of ocean waves conveys to the storm-tossed mariner. Have something to say; keep the fires of passion burning in your own soul; learn the real strength there is in the reserve of power; and the cultivated voice will not fail in its only legitimate office—that of making the clear and adequate impression of your thoughts and emotions upon the souls of others.

Elocutionary manuals properly devote much space to the consideration of gesture, for the eye should be addressed and pleased as well as the ear. But we doubt whether the marking out of special gestures to be imitated can do much good. A few broad principles like those formulated by the celebrated French teacher, Delsarte, may be profitably studied and made familiar by practice upon a few simple selections. After that the principal use of training is to give confidence so that the speaker may be in the full possession and instinctive use of all his powers. Fear often freezes the speaker into ice-like rigidity; and hearers are apt to feel the same deadly chill when listening to some one whose dominating sentiment is the fear that he may do something ridiculous, or fail to win their favor.

The secondary use of training in gesture is to discard awkward and repulsive movements. Timidity and fear may be overcome by a firm resolution, and the object is well worth the effort. Bad or ungraceful actions are far better in the case of a beginner than no action at all. The saying of Demosthenes, that the first, the second, and the third need of an orator is "ACTION," does not fully apply to the modern speaker. He needs many things more urgently than action, even when that word is taken in its widest sense. But action is important, and when graceful and expressive, it does powerfully tend to arrest attention, and even to help the processes of thought on the part of the speaker himself. We have heard several eloquent men who scarcely moved during the delivery of an address, but never without feeling that good gesticulation would have been a great addition to their power. It is unnatural to speak for any considerable period of time without moving. None but a lazy, sick, or bashful man will do it. Let the laziness be shaken off, the sickness cured, and the bashfulness reserved for a more fitting occasion! A man who is too bashful and diffident to move hand, head, or foot in the presence of an audience should in consistency refuse to monopolize their time at all!

Practice will usually overcome this fault. When a man has stood a great many times before an audience without receiving any serious injury, and has a good purpose in thus claiming their attention, and something which he thinks they ought to hear, he will forget his fears and allow his mind to be engrossed, as that of a true speaker should be, with the subject he has in hand. Then all his gestures will have at least the grace of unconscious and spontaneous origination.

But when fear has been overcome so that the speaker is not afraid to use his hands, he needs to enter upon a determined and comprehensive campaign against bad habits. If anything is truly natural—that is, true to the higher or universal nature—it will be beautiful; but early examples are so often wrong and corrupting that it is hard to say what nature is: Nature may be a bad nature—the reflection of all that is low and sordid as well as that which is high and ennobling. That nature which is in harmony with the sum of all things, which is the image of the Creator's perfectness, must be right and good; but we must not too hastily conclude that any habits of our own have this high and unquestionable source. Hardly a speaker lives who does not at some time fall into unsightly or ridiculous habits. The difference between men in this respect is that some steadily accumulate all the faults they ever have contracted, until the result is most repulsive; while others, from the warnings of friends or their own observation, discover their errors and cast them off.

A mode by which the solitary student may become acquainted with his faults, and from which he should not be driven by foolish ridicule, is by declaiming in as natural and forcible a manner as possible before a large mirror. Thus we may "see ourselves as others see us." Repeated practice in this manner will enable you to keep the necessary watch upon your motions, without so much distracting attention as to make the exercise before the glass no trustworthy specimen of ordinary habits. In speaking, you hear your own voice and thus become sensible of audible errors, but the glass is required to show improper movements that may have been unconsciously contracted. It is not advised that each speech, before delivery, should be practiced in front of the mirror. It is doubtful if such practice would not cherish a self-consciousness worse than all the errors it corrected. But the same objection would not apply to occasional declamations made for the very purpose of self-criticism.

By these two processes—pressing out into action as freely as possible under the impulse of deep feeling, and by lopping off everything that is not graceful and effective—we may soon attain a good style of gesture. When the habit of suiting the action to the word is once fully formed, all anxiety on that subject may be dismissed. The best gesticulation is entirely unconscious.

CHAPTER X

CONFIDENCE

How may that boldness and confidence which is indispensable to an orator best be acquired? On your success in this direction, hinges all other kinds of improvement. So long as a nervous dread hangs about you, it will make the practice of extemporaneous speech painful and repulsive, paralyzing all your faculties in the moment of utterance.

You must acquire confidence in your own powers and be willing to trust to their guidance.

But it is not necessary that you should exhibit or even feel this confidence at the beginning of a speech, for it may then appear like boastfulness or egotism. It is enough if you then have confidence in your subject, and in the fullness of your preparation. You may then without injury wish that some one, that you imagine more worthy, stood in your place. But if this feeling continues all through the address, failure is inevitable. Many a man begins while trembling in every limb, especially if the occasion be of unusual character, but soon becomes inspired with his theme and forgets all anxiety. If your fear be greater and more persistent, keeping you in perpetual terror, it will destroy all liberty and eloquence. When laboring under such an influence, you lose self-possession, become confused, all interest evaporates from your most carefully prepared thoughts, and you sit down at length, convinced that you have failed. It is but little consolation to believe that you had all the time in your brain the necessary power and material to achieve splendid success, if you had but possessed the courage to use it aright.

There is no remedy for fear more effectual than to do all our work under the immediate inspiration of duty. This feeling is not the privilege of the minister alone, but of each one who is conscious that he occupies the place where he stands because it is his right to be there, because he has some information to give, some cause to advocate, or some important task to do. With such consciousness we can speak our best, and finish with the satisfaction of having done our work as truly as if we had performed duty placed upon us in any other department of labor. But if we aim simply at making an exhibition of self and of showing our own skill and eloquence, then the smiles and frowns of the audience becomes a matter of overwhelming importance, and if we fail we are deeply mortified and bewail our foolishness in exposing ourselves to such needless risk.

The lack of proper confidence is the great reason for using manuscript in the moment of speech. The speaker makes one effort to extemporize and fails. This is not wonderful, for the path to success usually lies through failure from the time that we master the wonderful art of walking through many failures; but instead of copying the schoolboy motto, "try, try again," and reaping wisdom and experience from past efforts, he loses all hope—concludes that he is disqualified for that kind of work, and thus sinks to mediocrity and tameness, when he might have been brilliant in the fields of true oratory.

The exhibition of confidence and resolution by the speaker is a draft drawn on the respect of an audience which is nearly always honored, while the opposite qualities hide the possession of real talent. Hearers readily pardon timidity at the beginning of an address, for then attention is fixed upon the speaker himself, and his shrinking seems a graceful exhibition of modesty. But when he has fully placed his subject before them they associate him with it. If he is dignified and assured, they listen in pleased attention and acknowledge the weight of his words. These qualities are very different from bluster and bravado, which injure the cause advocated and excite disgust toward the speaker. The first appears to arise from a sense of the dignity of the subject; the second, from an assumption of personal superiority—an opinion no speaker has a right to entertain, for in the very act of addressing an audience he constitutes them his judges.

An orator needs confidence in his own powers in order to avail himself fully of the suggestions of the moment. Some of the best thoughts he will ever think flash upon him while speaking, and are out of the line of his preparation. There is no time to carefully weigh them.

He must reject them immediately or begin to follow, not knowing whither they lead, and this in audible words, with the risk that he may be landed in some absurdity. He cannot pause for a moment, as the least hesitation breaks the spell he has woven around his hearers, while if he rejects the offered idea he may lose a genuine inspiration. One searching glance that will not allow time for his own feelings or those of his auditors to cool, and then—decision to reject, or to follow the new track with the same assurance as if the end were clearly in view—this is all that is possible. It requires some boldness to pursue the latter course, and yet every speaker knows that his highest efforts—efforts that have seemed beyond his normal power, and which have done more in a minute to gain the object for which he spoke than all the remainder of the discourse—have been of this character.

It also requires a good degree of confidence to firmly begin a sentence, even when the general idea is plain, without knowing just how it will end. This difficulty is experienced sometimes even by the most fluent. A man may learn to cast sentences very rapidly, but it will take a little time to pass them through his mind, and when one is finished, the next may not yet have fully condensed itself into words. To begin to utter a partially constructed sentence, uncertain how it will end, and press on without letting the people see any hesitation, demands no small confidence in one's power of commanding words and framing sentences. Yet a bold and confident speaker need feel no uneasiness. He may prolong a pause while he is thinking of a needed word, or throw in something extraneous to fill up the time till the right term and construction are found. Yet the perfect remedy for these dangers is to learn the difficult art of standing before an audience with nothing to say and making the pause as effective as any phase of speech. This can be done, dangerous as it seems. It does require far more of courage to face an audience when the mouth is empty than when we are talking; the mettle of troops is never so severely tried as when their cartridge-boxes are empty; but all the resources of eloquence are not at command until this test can be calmly and successfully endured. An eminent speaker once said to a friend after a very successful effort, "What part of the address you have been praising most impressed you?" "It was not anything you said," was the reply, "but the thrilling pause you made of nearly half a minute after a bold assertion, as if you were challenging any one to rise and deny what you had asserted." "Oh! I remember," returned the other; "I could not get the next sentence fixed quite right, and was fully determined not to say it at all unless it came into the proper shape."

This necessary confidence can be cultivated by striving to exercise it, and by assuming its appearance where the reality is not. The raw recruit is transformed into a veteran soldier by meeting and overcoming danger. All the drill in the world will not supply the want of actual experience on the battle-field. So the extempore speaker must make up his mind to accept all the risk, and patiently endure all the failures and perils that result. If he fully decides that the reward is worthy of the effort he will be greatly aided in the attempt, as he will thus avoid the wavering and shrinking and questioning that would otherwise distress him and paralyze his powers. A failure will but lead to stronger and more persistent effort, made with added experience. Success will be an argument for future confidence, and thus any result will forward him on his course.

In regard to the difficulty of framing sentences in the moment of utterance, the experienced speaker will become so expert, having found his way through so many difficulties of that kind, that the greatest danger experienced will be that of carelessly allowing his words to flow on without unity or polish. It does require a determined effort, not merely to express meaning, but to pack and compress the greatest possible amount into striking and crystalline words. Experience also gives him such a knowledge of the working of his own thoughts that he will be able to decide at the first suggestion what unbidden ideas should be accepted and what ones should be rejected. If these new thoughts, however far outside of his preparation, seem worthy, he will give them instant expression; if not, he will dismiss them and continue unchecked along his intended route.

It is hoped that the reading of this treatise will increase the confidence of extempore speakers in two ways; first, by producing in the mind of each one perfect conviction that for him the better way is to adopt unwritten speech without reserve; and second, by pointing out a mode of preparation which will give as good ground for confidence as a fully written manuscript could possibly supply. To gain confidence which is not warranted by the event would only provoke a hurtful reaction; but confidence which is justified by experience grows ever stronger.

We have thus glanced at a few of the qualities which need to be cultivated and strengthened for the purposes of public speech. The survey does not cover the whole field of desirable qualities, for this would be to give a treatise on general education. Perfect speech requires every faculty of the mind to be brought to the highest state of efficiency. There is no mental power which will not contribute to success. The whole limits of possible education are comprised in the two branches already mentioned as concerning the orator—those relating to the reception of knowledge and those to its communication. The harmonious combination and perfect development of these two is the ideal of excellence—an ideal so high that it can only be approached. All knowledge is of use to the orator. He may not have occasion to employ it in a particular speech, but it contributes to give certainty, breadth, and scope to his views, and assures him that what he does put into his speeches is the best that can be selected. If he is ignorant, he is obliged to use for a discourse on any subject not that material which is the best in itself, but simply the best that may happen to be known to him, and he cannot be sure that something far more suitable is not overlooked.

The communicating faculties are, if possible, still more important. A great part of the value even of a diamond depends upon its polish and setting, and the richest and wisest thoughts fail to reach the heart or captivate the intellect unless they are cast into the proper form, and given external beauty.

Let the speaker, then, have no fear of knowing too much. Neither need he despair if he does not now know a great deal. He cannot be perfect at once, but must build for future years. If he wishes a sudden and local celebrity that will never widen, but will probably molder away even in his own lifetime, he may possibly gain it in another way. Let him learn a few of the externals of elocution, and then, with great care, or by the free use of the materials of others, prepare a few finely worded discourses, and recite or declaim them over and over again as often as he can find a new audience. He may not gain as much applause as he desires by this method, but it will be sufficiently evanescent. He will not grow up to the measure of real greatness, but become daily more dwarfed and stereotyped in intellect.

The following quotation contains a good example of the seductive but misleading methods sometimes held up before the young orator: "They talk," said Tom Marshall to an intimate friend, "of my astonishing bursts of eloquence, and doubtless imagine it is my genius bubbling over. It is nothing of the sort. I'll tell you how I do it: I select a subject and study it from the ground up. When I have mastered it fully, I write a speech on it. Then I take a walk and come back, and revise and correct. In a few days I subject it to another pruning, and then recopy it. Next I add the finishing touches, round it off with graceful periods, and commit it to memory. Then I speak it in the fields, in my father's lawn, and before my mirror, until gesture and delivery are perfect. It sometimes takes me six weeks or two months to get up a speech. When I am prepared I come to town. I generally select a court day, when there is sure to be a crowd. I am called on for a speech, and am permitted to select my own subject. I speak my piece. It astonishes the people, as I intended it should, and they go away marveling at my power of oratory. They call it genius, but it is the hardest kind of work."

No objection is made to the quantity of work thus described, but might not the same amount be expended in more profitable directions? A speech thus prepared was a mere trick intended to astonish the people. Sometimes the great Daniel Webster took equal pains in the verbal expression of some worthy thought, which was afterward held in the grasp of a powerful memory until a fitting place was found for it in some masterly speech. The difference between the two processes is greater than seems at first glance. Marshall's plan was like a beautiful garment thrown over a clothes dummy in a shop window; Webster's, like the same garment, worn for comfort and ornament by a living man.

It is better that the speaker should "intermeddle with all knowledge," and make the means of communicating his thoughts as perfect as possible. Then out of the fullness of his treasure, let him talk to the people with an adequate purpose in view, and if no sudden acclaim greets him, he will be weighty and influential from the first, and each passing year will add to his power.

CHAPTER XI

The Pen and the Tongue

It does not follow from anything we have said that the pen should be discarded by the extempore speaker. Because he is not obliged to write each word, he should not feel excused from writing altogether. Few greater misfortunes could happen to a speaker than being deprived of the power of recording and preserving notes for the purposes of oratory. The most tenacious memory is burdened by the weight of a large number of intended discourses, especially if they are long and complex. No person can feel sure that he will remember all parts of the speech he intended to utter even in outline, unless it has been reduced to regular form so that one part will suggest another. In going to a store to purchase a few articles the pen is very useful in making a memorandum; if the errand boy neglects that precaution some of the most essential things may be forgotten. Among illiterate people a great many mnemonic signs have been employed, such as associating things to be remembered with the fingers, etc.; but among intelligent persons all of these have been superseded by the use of writing, and it would be very absurd to advocate a return to the old modes on the plea that the memory might be so strengthened that all items could be safely remembered. The reply would be ready: "Yes, it is possible; but we have a far better and less burdensome way of accomplishing the same object and have no motive in returning to the more difficult mode." Thus while it may be possible to arrange in the mind all the outlines of a long discourse, it is not easy to do it, and there is no gain in the extra labor involved. Everything bearing upon a discourse may be written in brief outline, and then a selection made of what is best, throwing out all other portions. The remainder can then be far better arranged when in such a position that the eye as well as the mind can glance at it. The preparation for the intended speech thus assumes the shape of a miniature or outline, and may be filled out at any point which needs strengthening.

But even if it were possible to construct the plan and speak well without any previous use of the pen, this would, in the majority of cases, be insufficient. The orator needs to preserve the materials, if not the form of his oration, either for use in future speeches or for comparison with later efforts. It is very wasteful to throw away valuable material once accumulated, and then search the same ground over again when required to treat the same topic. This would be acting in the spirit of the savage who eats enough to satisfy his appetite and throws away all that remains, as he feels no further need for it, and only begins to gather again when hunger spurs him to exertion.

The pen is the instrument of accumulation and preservation, and should be diligently employed. No speaker can rise to permanent greatness without it. The instances given to the contrary are mere delusions or evasions. If the service of other pens can be employed, as in the case of shorthand reporters and amanuenses, this is but doing the same thing under another form.

The principal purpose of the chapters that follow is to show how the pen may be used in such a manner as to preserve and arrange all the material we may gather, elaborate, or originate on any subject, so as to bring to the moment of unfettered extempore speech all the certainty of result and accumulated power of which our faculties are capable.

Bacon says: "Reading makes a full man, writing an exact man, and conference a ready man." All these means should be used and all these qualities attained by the eloquent speaker.

CHAPTER XII

SUBJECT AND OBJECT

We now enter upon the most practical part of our subject. We have seen what natural qualities are indispensable, and how these, when possessed, can be improved by training. The importance of a wide scope of knowledge bearing upon oratory, and of understanding and having some command of the powers of language has been pointed out. When a man has all of these, and is still a diligent student growing daily in knowledge, he is ready to consider the methods by which all his gifts and acquirements may be concentrated upon a single speech. Some of the directions in this and the immediately succeeding chapters are of universal application, while others are thrown out as mere suggestions to be modified and changed according to individual taste or particular circumstances.

A plan is necessary for every kind of speech. A rude mass of brick, lumber, mortar, and iron, thrown together as the materials chance to be furnished, does not constitute a house until each item is built into its own place according to some intelligent design. A speech has the same need of organization. A few minutes of desultory talk, whether uttered in a low or high voice, to one person or to many, does not make a speech. The talk may be good, or useful, or striking: it may be replete with sparkling imagery, and full of valuable ideas that command attention, and yet be no real discourse. The question, "What was all this about? what end did the speaker have in view?" is a fatal condemnation. The subject and object of every discourse should be perfectly obvious—if not at the opening, surely at the close of the address. The only safe method is to have a well-defined plan marked out from beginning to end, and then to bring every part of the work into subordination to one leading idea. The plan itself should be constructed with some clear object in view.

It is better that this construction of the plan should be completed before delivery begins. If you are suddenly called to speak on some topic you have often thought over, the whole outline of the address, with a plan perfect in every part, may flash upon you in a moment, and you may speak as well as if you had been allowed months for preparation. But such cases are rare exceptions. The man who attempts, on the spur of the moment, to arrange his facts, draw his inferences, and enforce his opinions, will usually find the task very difficult, even if the topic is within his mental grasp, and his memory promptly furnishes him with all necessary materials.

We will now consider the subject and object which every true discourse, whatever its character, must possess.

First, as to the object: why is it that at a particular time an audience assembles and sits in silence, while one man standing up, talks to them? What is his motive in thus claiming their attention? Many of them may have come from mere impulse, of which they could give no rational explanation, but the speaker at least should have a definite purpose.

A clear aim tends powerfully to give unity and consistency to the whole discourse, and to prevent him from wandering into endless digressions. It binds all detached parts together and infuses a common life through his address. Such a ruling aim cannot be too definitely recognized and carefully kept in view, for it is the foundation of the whole discourse.

This object should not be too general in character. It is not enough that we wish to please or to do good: it may be safely assumed that speakers generally wish to do both. But how shall these ends be reached? "What special good do I hope to accomplish by this address?"

When you have made the object definite, you are better prepared to adapt all available means to its accomplishment. It should also be stated that the more objects are subdivided the more precision will be augmented, though there is a limit beyond which such division would be at the expense of other qualities.

Your object will usually have reference to the opinion or the action of those addressed, and the firmer your own conviction of the truth of that opinion, or the desirableness of that action, the greater, other things being equal, your persuasive power will be. If you do not know exactly what you wish, there is little probability that your audience will care to interpret your thought; they will take it for granted that you really mean nothing, and even if you do incidentally present some truth supported by good arguments, they will consider it a matter not calling for any immediate consideration or definite decision on their part.

The speaker's objects are comparatively few and are often determined by his very position and employment. If you are engaged in a political canvass you are seeking to confirm and retain the votes of your own party, while persuading over to your side the opposition. Votes constitute the object you seek, and to win them is your purpose. But there are many ways by which that desirable end may be accomplished—some wise and noble, others ignoble. But a political orator will gain in power by keeping clearly in view his purpose and rejecting from his speeches all things that merely arouse and embitter opponents, without, at the same time, contributing to strengthen the hold of the speaker's own party upon its members.

If you are a lawyer you wish to win your case. The judge's charge, the jury's verdict, are your objective points, and all mere display which does not contribute directly or indirectly to these ends is worse than wasted, as it may even interfere with your real purpose.

Much of your success will depend upon keeping the right object before you at the right time. If you aim at that which is unattainable, the effort is not only lost, but the object which you could have reached may in the meantime have passed out of your reach. Everybody has heard ministers arguing against some forms of unbelief which their hearers know nothing about. This is worse than useless; it may suggest the very errors intended to be refuted; and if this does not result, to think that the refutation will be stored up until the time when the errors themselves may be encountered, is to take a most flattering view of the length of time during which sermons as well as other discourses are remembered. You may avoid these errors by selecting some object which is practicable at the moment of utterance: the first right step makes all after success possible.

There is a difference between the object of a speech and its subject; the former is the motive that impels us to speak, while the latter is what we speak about. It is not uncommon for talkers to have a subject without any definite object, unless it be the very general one of complying with a form or fulfilling an engagement. When the period for the talk comes—it would not be right to call it a speech—they take the easiest subject they can find, express all the ideas they happen to have about it, and leave the matter. Until such persons become in earnest, and get a living object, true eloquence is utterly impossible.

The object of a discourse is the soul, while the subject is but the body; or, as we may say, the one is the end, while the other is the means by which it is accomplished. After the object is clearly realized by the speaker, he can choose the subject to much better advantage. It may happen that one object is so much more important than all other practicable ones that it forces itself irresistibly on his attention and thus saves the labor of choice; at other times he may have several different objects with no particular reason for preferring one of them in the order of time to another. In this case if a subject fills his mind it will be well to discuss it with an aim toward the object which may be best enforced by its means.

After all, it makes but little difference which of these two is chosen first. It is enough that when you undertake to speak you have a subject you fully understand, and an object that warms your heart and enlists all your powers. You can then speak, not as one who deals with abstractions, but as having a living mission to perform.

It is important that each subject should be complete in itself, and rounded off from everything else. Its boundaries should be run with such precision as to include all that belongs to it, but nothing more. It is a common but grievous fault to have the same cast of ideas flowing around every subject. There are few things in the universe which have not some relation to everything else. If we do not, therefore, very strictly bound our subject, we will find ourselves bringing the same matter into each discourse and perpetually repeating our thoughts. If ingenious in that matter, we may find a good excuse for getting our favorite anecdotes and brilliant ideas into connection with the most opposite kinds of subjects. An old minister once gave me an amusing account of the manner in which he made outlines of the sermons of a local celebrity. The first one was a very able discourse, with three principal divisions—man's fallen estate, the glorious means provided for his recovery, and the fearful consequences of neglecting those means. Liking the sermon very well, my informant went to hear the same man again. The text was new, but the first proposition, was *man's fallen estate*; the second, the glorious means provided for his recovery; and the last, the fearful consequences of neglecting those means. Thinking that the repetition was an accident, another trial was made. The text was at as great a remove as possible from the other two. The first proposition was, man's fallen estate; and the others followed in due order. This was an extreme instance of a common fault, which is by no means confined to the ministry. When an eloquent Congressman was once delivering a great address, a member on the opposite benches rubbed his hands in apparently ecstatic delight, and remarked in a stage whisper, "Oh! how I have always loved to hear that speech!" In a book of widely circulated sermon sketches, nearly every one begins by asserting that man has fallen and needs the helps or is liable to the evils mentioned afterward. No doubt this primary statement is important, but it might sometimes be taken for granted. The fault which we have here pointed out is not uncommon in preaching. Occasionally ministers acquire such a stereotyped form of expression that what they say in one sermon is sure to recur, perhaps in a modified form, in all others. This is intolerable. There is an end to the patience of man. He tires of the same old ideas, and wishes, when a new text is taken, that it may bring with it some novelty in the sermon. The remedy against the evil under consideration is found in the careful selection and definition of subjects. Give to each its own territory and guard rigidly against all trespassers. A speaker should not only see that what he says has some kind of connection with the subject in hand, but that it has a closer connection with that subject than any other he may be called upon to discuss at or near the same time. A very great lecturer advertises a number of lectures upon topics that seem to be totally independent. Yet all the lectures are but one, except a few paragraphs in the introduction of each. This is really a less fault in the case of an itinerating lecturer than in most other fields of oratory, as the same people hear the lecture but once. Yet even then the false assumption of intellectual riches implied in the numerous titles cannot be justified.

The subject should be so well defined that we always know just what we are speaking about. It may be of a general nature, but our knowledge of it should be clear and adequate. This is more necessary in an extempore than in a written speech, though the want of it will be severely felt in the latter also. A strong, vividly defined subject will give unity to the whole discourse, and probably leave a permanent impression on the mind of the hearer. To aid in securing this it will be well to reduce every subject to its simplest form, and then, by writing it as a compact phrase or sentence, stamp it on the mind, and let it ring in every utterance; that is, let each word aid in carrying out the central idea, or in leading up to it. Those interminable discourses that begin anywhere and lead nowhere, may be called speeches or sermons, by courtesy, but they are not such.

To always preserve this unity of theme and treatment is not easy, and calls, often, for the exercise of heroic self-denial. To see in the mind's eye what we know would please and delight listeners, pander to their prejudices, or gain uproarious applause, and then turn away with the words unspoken, merely because it is foreign to our subject—this is as sore a trial as for a miser on a sinking ship to abandon his gold. But it is equally necessary, if we would not fall into grave rhetorical errors. Any speech which is constructed on the plan of putting into it all the wise or witty or pleasing things the speaker can think of will be a mere mass of more or less foolish talk. Shakespeare is often reproached with having neglected the dramatic unities of place and time; but he never overlooked the higher unities of subject and object. These remarks do not imply that illustration should be discarded or even used sparingly. The whole realm of nature may be ransacked for these gems, and if they do illustrate, they are often better than statement or argument. If the thing to be illustrated belongs to the subject, then every apt illustration of it also belongs there.

It is possible that men of genius may neglect the unity of subject and object, and still succeed by sheer intellectual force, as they might do under any other circumstances. But ordinary men cannot with safety follow the example of Sidney Smith. His hearers complained that he did not "stick to his text," and, that he might reform the more easily, they suggested that he should divide his sermons as other ministers did. He promised to gratify them, and the next Sabbath, after reading his text, he began: "We will divide our discourse this morning into three parts: in the first place, we will go *up* to our text; in the second place, we will go *through* it; and in the third place, we will go *from* it." There was general agreement that he succeeded best on the last head, but preachers who are not confident of possessing his genius had better confine themselves to the former two.

A true discourse is the orderly development of some one thought or idea with so much clearness and power that it may ever after live as a point of light in the memory. Other ideas may cluster around the central one, but it must reign supreme. If the discourse fails in this particular nothing else can redeem it. Brilliancy of thought and illustration will be as completely wasted as a sculptor's art on a block of clay.

A man of profound genius once arose to preach before a great assemblage, and every breath was hushed. He spoke with power, and many of his passages were of thrilling eloquence. He poured forth beautiful images and solemn thoughts with the utmost profusion; yet when at the end of an hour he took his seat, the prevailing sentiment was one of disappointment. The address was confused—utterly destitute of any point of union to which the memory could cling. Many of his statements were clear and impressive, but he did not make evident what he was talking about. It was an impressive warning against erecting a building before laying a foundation.

CHAPTER XIII

Thought - Gathering

After the subject upon which we are to speak has been determined the logical order of preparation is, first, gathering material; second, selecting what is most fitting and arranging the whole into perfect order; third, fixing this in the mind so that it may be available for the moment of use. These processes are not always separated in practice, but they may be best considered in the order indicated.

When a subject is chosen and the mind fastened upon it, that subject becomes a center of attraction and naturally draws all kindred ideas toward it. Old memories that had become dim from the lapse of time are slowly hunted out and grouped around the parent thought. Each hour of contemplation that elapses, even if there is not direct study, adds to the richness and variety of our available mental stores. The relations between different and widely separated truths become visible, just as new stars are seen when we gaze intently toward the evening sky. All that lies within our knowledge is subjected to a rigid scrutiny and all that appears to have any connection with the subject is brought into view. Usually a considerable period of time is needed for this process, and the longer it is continued the better, if interest in the subject is not suffered to decline in the meanwhile.

But it is somewhat difficult to continue at this work long enough without weariness. The capacity for great and continuous reaches of thought constitutes a principal element in the superiority of one mind over another. Even the mightiest genius cannot, at a single impulse, exhaust the ocean of truth that opens around every object of man's contemplation. It is only by viewing a subject in every aspect that superficial and one-sided impressions can be guarded against. But the continuous exertion and toil this implies are nearly always distasteful, and the majority of men can only accomplish it by a stern resolve. Whether acquired or natural, the ability to completely "think out" a subject is of prime necessity; the young student at the outset should learn to finish every investigation he begins and continue the habit during life. Doing this or not doing it will generally be decisive of his success or failure from an intellectual point of view. Thought is a mighty architect, and if you keep him fully employed, he will build up with slow and measured strokes a gorgeous edifice upon any territory at all within your mental range. You may weary of his labor and think that the wall rises so slowly that it will never be completed; but wait. In due time, if you are patient, all will be finished and will then stand as no ephemeral structure, to be swept away by the first storm that blows, but will be established and unshaken on the basis of eternal truth.

M. Bautain compares the accumulation of thought around a subject upon which the mind thus dwells with the development of organic life by continuous growth from an almost imperceptible germ. Striking as is the analogy, there is one point of marked dissimilarity. This growth of thought is voluntary and may easily be arrested at any stage. The introduction of a new subject or cessation of effort on the old is fatal. To prevent this and keep the mind employed until its work is done requires with most persons a regular and formal system. Profound thinkers, who take up a subject and cannot leave it until it is traced into all its intricate relations and comprehended in every part, and who have at the same time the power of easily recalling long trains of thought that have once passed through their mind, have less need of an artificial method. But their case is not that of the majority of thinkers or speakers.

We will give a method found useful for securing abundant speech materials, and allow others to adopt it as far as it may prove advantageous to them.

The things we actually know are not always kept equally in view. Sometimes we may see an idea with great clearness and after a time lose it again, while another, at first invisible, comes into sight. Each idea should be secured when it occurs. Let each thought that arises on the subject you intend to discuss be noted. A word or a brief sentence sufficient to recall the conception to your own mind will be enough, and no labor need be expended on composition or expression. After this first gathering, let the paper be laid aside and the subject be recommitted to the mind for further reflection. As other ideas arise let them be noted down in the same manner and the process be thus continued for days together. Sometimes new images and conceptions will continue to float into the mind for weeks. Most persons who have not tried this process of accumulation will be surprised to find how many thoughts they have on the simplest topic. If some of this gathered matter remains vague and shadowy, it will only be necessary to give it more time and more earnest thought and all obscurity will vanish.

At last there comes the consciousness that the mind's power on that particular theme is exhausted. If we also feel that we have all the material needed, one step further only remains in this part of the work; the comparison of our treasures with what others have accomplished in the same field. It may be that this comparison will show the worthlessness of much of our own material, but it is better to submit to the humiliation involved and be sure that we have the best that can be furnished by other minds as well as our own. If we prefer, we may speak when we have gathered only the materials that are already within our own grasp and thus have a greater consciousness of originality, but such consciousness is a delusion unless based upon exhaustive research. Nearly all that we thus gather will be the result of previous reading, and almost the only thing in its favor over the fresh accumulations that we make by reading directly in the line of our subject, is the probability that the former knowledge will be better digested.

But more frequently, after the young orator has recollected and briefly noted all that bears upon his subject with which his own mind furnishes him, there remains a sense of incompleteness, and he is driven to seek a further supply. He is now hungry for new information, and on this state there is an intellectual blessing corresponding to the moral blessing pronounced upon those who hunger and thirst after righteousness. He reads the works of those who have treated the same or related topics, converses with well-informed persons, observes the world closely, still putting down every new idea that seems to bear upon his theme. Whenever an idea is found which supplies a felt want, it is received with great joy. It often happens that instead of finding the very thing sought for he strikes upon the first link of some chain of thoughts in his own mind that leads up to what he desires, but has hitherto overlooked. The new idea is only the more valued when it has thus been traced out.

Now, we have on paper, and often after much toil, a number of confused, unarranged notes. They are destitute of polish, and no more constitute a speech than the piles of brick and lumber a builder accumulates constitute a house. Indeed, this comparison is too favorable, for the builder has carefully calculated just what he needs for his house, and has ordered those very things. But usually we have in our notes much that can be of no use, and at whatever sacrifice of feeling it must be thrown out. This is a matter of great importance. It has been said that the principal difference between the conversation of a wise man and of a fool is that the one speaks all that is in his mind, while the other gives utterance only to carefully selected thoughts. Nearly all men have at times ideas that would please and profit any audience; and if these are carefully weeded out from the puerilities by which they may be surrounded, the remainder will be far more valuable than the whole mass. Everything not in harmony with the controlling object or purpose must be thrown away at whatever sacrifice of feeling. Read carefully your scattered notes after the fervor of pursuit has subsided and erase every phrase that is unfitting. If but little remains you can continue the search as at first, and erase and search again, until you have all that you need of matter truly relevant to the subject. Yet it is not well to be over-fastidious. This would prevent speech altogether, or make the work of preparation so slow and wearisome that when the hour of effort arrived, all freshness and vigor would be gone. A knight in Spenser's "Faery Queen" entered an enchanted castle and as he passed through eleven rooms in succession he saw written on the walls of each the words, "Be bold;" but on the twelfth the inscription changed to the advice of equal wisdom, "Be not too bold." The same injunctions are appropriate to the orator. He should be careful in the selection of his material, but not too careful. Many things which a finical taste might reject are allowable and very effective. No definite rule, however, can be given on the subject, as it is a matter of taste rather than of calculation.

CHAPTER XIV

Constructing a Plan

The thoughts which have been gathered in the modes pointed out in the last chapter are now to be arranged in the most effective order. It will not usually do to begin a speech with those things we happen to first think of, and proceed to others that are less obvious. This would lead to an anti-climax fatal to eloquence. A speaker who adopted this mode once complained that his speeches often seemed to taper to a very fine point, and that he lost all interest in them before finishing. The explanation was simple; he uttered first those thoughts which were familiar to himself and came afterward to those which had been sought out by more or less painful effort, and which seemed less certain and valuable. The remedy for this fault is found in careful arrangement. The most familiar thoughts will naturally be jotted down first, but it does not follow that they should occupy the same place in the finished plan of the speech.

The true mode of improving your plans is to bestow a great deal of time and thought upon them, and to make no disposition of any part for which you cannot give a satisfactory reason. This direction relates only to the beginner. In time the formation of plans will become so natural that any variation from the most effective arrangement will be felt as keenly as a discord in music is felt by a master in that art. From such carefully constructed plans, firm, coherent, and logical discourses will result.

There are certain general characteristics that each plan should possess. It must fully indicate the nature of the proposed discourse and mark out each of its successive steps with accuracy. Any want of definiteness in the outline is a fatal defect. You must feel that you can rely absolutely on it for guidance to the end of your discourse or be always in danger of embarrassment and confusion.

Each clause should express a distinct idea, and but one. This should be repeated in no other part of the discourse; otherwise, we fall into wearisome repetitions, the great vice, as it is often claimed, of extempore speakers.

A brief plan is better, other things being equal, than a long one. Often a single word will recall an idea as perfectly as many sentences, and it will burden the memory less. We do not expect the draft of a house to equal the house in size, but only to preserve a proportionate relation to it throughout. The plan cannot supply the thought, but, indicating what is in the mind, it shows how to bring it forth in regular succession. It is a pathway leading to a definite end, and, like all pathways, its crowning merits are directness and smoothness. Without these qualities it will perplex and hinder rather than aid. Each word in the plan should suggest an idea, and be so firmly bound to that idea that the two cannot become separated in any exigency of speech. You will find it sorely perplexing if, in the heat of discourse, some important note should lose the thought for which it previously stood and become an empty word. But with clear conceptions condensed into fitting words this cannot easily happen. A familiar idea can be expressed very briefly, while a strange or new conception may require more expansion. But all thoughts advanced by the speaker ought to be familiar to himself as the result of long meditation and thorough mastery, no matter how strange or startling they are to his hearers. Most skeletons may be brought within the compass of a hundred words, and every part be clearly indicated to the mind that conceived it, though perhaps not to any other.

There may be occasions when a speaker is justified in announcing his divisions and subdivisions, but such cases are exceptions. Hearers do not care how a discourse is constructed, so it comes to them warm and pulsating with life. To give the plan of a speech before the speech itself is contrary to the order of nature. We are not required first to look upon a grisly skeleton before we can see a graceful, living body. There is a skeleton inside each body, but during life it is well hidden, and there is no reason that the speaker should anticipate the work of the tomb. It is hardly less objectionable to name the parts of the discourse during the progress of the discussion, for—continuing the former illustration—bones that project through the skin are very unlovely. The only case, I presume to think, where it is justifiable to name the parts of a discourse, either before or during its delivery, is where the separate parts have an importance of their own, in addition to their office of contributing to the general object. Much of the proverbial "dryness" of sermons arises from the preacher telling what he is about to remark, firstly, before he actually makes the remark thus numbered. Whenever we hear a minister read his text, announce his theme, state the parts into which he means to divide it, and then warn us that the first head will be subdivided into a certain number of parts, each of which is also specified in advance, we prepare our endurance for a severe test.

CHAPTER XV

How Shall the Written Plan be Used?

Now that the plan is completed and fully written out, the next question arises as to what shall be done with it. It may either be used or abused. To read it to the audience or exhibit it to them would be an obvious abuse. Possibly if the speaker possessed a large blackboard, the latter course might, in special cases, have some advantages. But even then it is better that the students should, in most instances, exercise their own ingenuity in gathering out of the body of the speech the central thoughts which they wish to preserve in their notebooks, than that the work should be done for them in advance by having the whole plan of the lecture placed in their sight.

The writer has experimented on this subject by repeating the same lecture to different classes with the outline in some cases exposed to view, and in the others concealed: the interest has always seemed to be greater, and the understanding more complete in the latter case. If this is true where instruction is the only aim, it is still more necessary where persuasion is the object of the speaker. The exposing in advance of the means by which he intends to work, will put on their guard the very persons whose hearts he wishes to capture, and thus lose him all that advantage of surprise which is often as momentous in oratorical as in military affairs.

There are two other ways of using the plan to be considered. One is to keep it in the speaker's sight, so that he may step along from one item to another, thus keeping a foundation of written words in the midst of the uncertainty of his extemporaneous efforts, like that afforded by stepping-stones to a man crossing a running stream. There are some advantages in such use. The speaker will feel freer in making those pauses which are sometimes necessary for the sake of emphasis.

He is better able to collect his scattered ideas in case any untoward circumstance should break the thread of his discourse. If he is confused for a moment, he may look down to his paper and recover himself, while if thoughts and words flow easily he can ignore the plan which lies before him.

But all the reasons for thus using the plan are the most emphatic condemnation of the practice. They are all make-shifts. They are based upon the thought that the great object is to secure the speaker from danger and confusion; in other words, they put him on the defensive, instead of the aggressive. Were the question to be stated, "How can a man best preserve the form of extemporaneous speech while shielding himself from the most dangerous incidents of that mode of address?" it might plausibly be replied, "By making a very full plan and concealing it at some point within the reach of his eyes, and using it whenever that course becomes easiest."

But we have not sought to point out the mode of speech which will best protect the speaker from risks incident to his work. For real effectiveness, compromises are usually hurtful, and this expedient forms no exception.

To have a plan in sight tends powerfully to break up the speech into fragments and destroy its unity. A series of short addresses on related points, affords no substitute for a concentrated discourse. The speaker who publicly uses his sketch, speaks on until he reaches a point at which he does not know what is to come next, and on the brink of that gulf, looks down at his notes, and, perhaps after a search, finds what he wants. Had the thought existed in his mind, it would have blended the close of the preceding sentences into harmony with it. Direct address to the people, which they so much value in a speaker, is interfered with in the same way, for his eye must rest for a portion of the time upon his notes. He will also be apt to mention the divisions of his speech as they occur, because the eye is resting upon them at the same time the tongue is engaged, and it is hard to keep the two members from working in harmony.

If notes must be used the same advice applies that we have already offered to those who read in full. Be honest about it; do not try to hide the notes. Any attempt to prove to an audience that we are doing what we are not doing, has in it an element of deception, and is morally objectionable. The use of notes is not wrong, but to use them while pretending not to use them is wrong.

Some speakers carry their notes in their pockets for the sake of being able to take them out in case they find their memory failing, and thus they guard against the misfortune which once befell the eloquent Abbe Bautain, who, on ascending the pulpit to preach before the French King and Court, found that he had forgotten subject, plan, and text. This method is honest and unobjectionable, for the notes of the plan are either not used by the speaker at all, or if he takes them from his pocket, the people will understand the action.

The only remaining method, and that which we would urge upon every extempore speaker, is to commit the plan, as sketched, to memory. It is put in the best possible shape for the expression of the subject by the labor which has been previously bestowed upon it, and now such review as will give the mind a perfect recollection of the whole subject in its orderly unfolding is just what is needed for final mastery. Previously much of the work of preparation was given to detached fragments. Now the subject as a whole is spread out. The time given to a thorough memorizing of the plan need not be great; it will indeed be but small if the plan itself is so well arranged that every preceding part suggests what follows; but it will be the most fruitful of all the time spent in preparation. It puts you in the best condition for speaking. The object is then fixed in the heart and will fire it to earnestness and zeal, while the subject is spread, like a map, before the mental vision. All the power you possess can then be brought to bear directly upon the people. Do not fear that in the hurry of discourse you will forget some part of what is clear when you begin. If you are in good mental and physical condition, the act of speech will be exhilarating and stimulating, so that every fine line of preparation will come into clearness just at the right time, and many a relation unperceived before, many a forgotten fact, will spring up in complete and vivid perception. There is a wonderful luxury of feeling in such speech. Sailing with a swift wind, riding a race-horse, even the joy of victorious battle—indeed, all enjoyments that arise from the highest powers called forth into successful exercise—are inferior to the thrill and intoxication of the highest form of successful extemporaneous speech. To think of using notes then would seem like a contemptible impertinence! Imagine Xavier or Luther with their notes spread out before them, looking up the different items from which to address the multitudes spell-bound before them! The Presbyterian Deacon who once prayed in the presence of his note-using Pastor, "O Lord! teach Thy servants to speak from the heart to the heart, and not from a little piece of paper, as the manner of some is," was not so very far wrong!

It is advisable to commit the plan to memory a considerable time before speaking. It then takes more complete possession of the mind and there is less liability of forgetting some portion. This is less important when the subject is perfectly familiar, for then "out of the abundance of the heart the mouth speaketh," but those subjects which have been recently studied for the first time are in a different position; and some meditation upon that which has just been arranged in its best form will be very serviceable. Even if the salient points are firmly grasped, some of the minor parts may require further close consideration. No study is ever so profitable as that which is bestowed after the plan is complete, for up to that time there is danger that some of the thoughts to which our attention is given may be ultimately rejected and others radically modified. But when the plan is finished each idea has settled into its place. If obscurity rests anywhere, it may be detected at once, and the strength of the mind be brought to bear for its banishment. Impressions derived from meditation are then easily retained until the hour of speech, because associated with their proper place in the prepared outline. Such deep meditation on each division of the discourse can scarcely fail to make it original in the true sense of the term, and weave all its parts together with strong and massive thoughts.

After the plan has been memorized we can meditate upon it not only at the desk, but anywhere. As we walk about or lie in bed, or at any other time find our minds free from distractions, we can ponder the ideas that cluster around our subject until they grow perfectly familiar. Even when we are reading or thinking on other topics, brilliant thoughts will not unfrequently spring up, or those we possessed before take stronger and more definite outlines. All such gains can be held in memory without the use of the pen, because the plan furnishes a suitable place for them.

The course here described we would urge strongly upon the

consideration of the young speaker. If carefully followed, its results will be invaluable. Arrange the plan from which you are to speak as clearly as may be in the form of a brief sketch; turn it over and over again; ponder each idea and the manner of bringing it out; study the connection between all the parts until the whole from beginning to end appears perfectly plain and simple. So frequently has this mode of preparation been tested that its effectiveness is no longer a matter of experiment.

It is advantageous to grasp the whole subject, as early as possible, in a single idea—in the same manner in which the future tree is compressed within the germ from which it is to spring. Then this one thought will suggest the entire discourse to the speaker, and at its conclusion will be left clear and positive in the hearer's mind. For some acute auditors this may be less necessary. They are able to outrun a loose speaker, arrange his scattered fragments, supply his omissions, and arrive at the idea which has not yet formed itself clearly in his own mind. Such persons often honestly commend orators who are incomprehensible to the majority of their hearers. But the opinions of such auditors are an unsafe guide, for they form a very small minority of any assembly.

There is one further step which may sometimes precede the moment of speech with profit—the placing upon paper of a brief but connected sketch or statement of the whole discourse. If this is made in the ordinary writing there is danger that its slowness will make it more of a word-study than what it is intended to be—a test of ideas. A thorough mastery of shorthand, or the service of some one who has such mastery, will supply this defect. If the plan is well arranged there will be no pause in the most rapid composition, and if the whole discourse can at one effort be thrown into a dress of words there may be full assurance that the same thing can be accomplished still more easily and effectively when the additional stimulus of an audience is supplied. There should be no attempt, in the moment of speaking, to recall the very words used in writing, but the command of language will undoubtedly be greatly improved by having so recently used many of the terms that will be again required. Frequently there will be fine passages in the speech which you have thus struck off at white heat that you may be unwilling to forget, but it is better to make no effort to remember them, for you are almost sure to rise still higher in the moment of public delivery.

When this rapid writing is not available, a partial substitute for it may be found in writing in the ordinary hand a brief sketch or compact model of the whole discourse. You will be surprised to notice how short a compass will suffice for a discourse requiring an hour or more in delivery, without the omission of a single material thought. Such a sketch differs from the plan in clearly expressing all the ideas that underlie the coming speech, while the latter would be nearly unintelligible to any but its author. The one is only a few marks thrown out in the field of thought by which an intended pathway is indicated; the other is a very brief view of the thoughts themselves, without adornment or verbiage. Some speakers who might feel insecure in trusting the notes and hints of the plan would feel perfectly safe in enlarging upon a statement of their thoughts so brief that the whole sketch of the speech would not require more than three or four minutes to read. But this whole plan of writing, either in full or in brief, is only an expedient, and need not be adopted by those who have full confidence in their trained and cultivated powers.

After you have prepared your plan it is well to preserve it for future use, which may be done by copying it into a book kept for that purpose: or, what is more convenient in practice, folding the slip of paper on which it is written into an envelope of suitable size with the subject written on the back. These may be classified and preserved, even in very large numbers, so as to be easily consulted. From time to time, as your ability grows, they may be improved upon so as to remain the complete expression of your ability on every theme treated. On the back of the envelope may also be written references to any source of additional information on the same subject, and printed or written scraps, valuable as illustrations, or for additional information, may be slipped inside.

CHAPTER XVI

The First Moment of Speech

Having completed all your preparations, you now anxiously await the commencement of the intellectual battle. This period is often a severe trial. Men who are physically brave sometimes tremble in anticipation of speedily standing before an audience. The shame of failure then may appear worse than death itself. As the soldier feels more of cold and shrinking terror when listening for the peal of the first gun, than afterward, when the conflict deepens into blood around him, so the speaker usually suffers more in this moment of expectancy than in any that follows. You behold the danger in its full magnitude, without the inspiration that attends it. Yet whatever effort it may cost, you must remain calm and collected, for if not master of yourself, you cannot expect to rule others. Your material must be kept well in hand, ready to be used at the proper time, though it is not well to be continually conning over your preparation. That would destroy the freshness of your matter and bring you to the decisive test weary and jaded. You only need such an occasional glance as will assure you that all your material remains within reach. It is seldom possible by any means to banish all fear, and it is to the speaker's advantage that he cannot. His timidity arises from several causes, which differ widely in the effects they produce. A conscious want of preparation, especially when this arises from any neglect or indolence, is one of the most distressing sources of fear. A species of remorse then mingles with the embarrassment natural to the moment. If the speaker has no other motive than to win reputation—to minister to his own vanity—he will feel terrified, as he realizes that shame instead of honor may be the result of his rashness. That man is fortunate who can say, "I only speak because I feel it to be duty which I dare not refuse—a work that I must perform whether well or ill." The lawyer who must defend his client, the minister who feels that the hour of service has arrived, the teacher in the presence of his class, are examples of those who speak under the same kind of compulsion that calls a field laborer out into the burning heat of a July noon whether he feels like it or not. But if you are about to speak because you have intruded into the work that properly belongs to another, you need to be very sure of your preparation, for in case of failure you will not have even your own sympathy.

But the most formidable and common foe of the speaker's, in these preliminary moments, is a general dread that can neither be analyzed nor accounted for. Persons who have never felt its power sometimes make light of it, but experience will change their views. The soldier who has never witnessed a battle, or felt the air throb with the explosion of cannon, or heard the awful cries of the wounded, is often a great braggart; while "the scarred veteran of a hundred fights" never speaks of the carnival of blood without shuddering, and would be the last, but for the call of duty, to brave the danger he knows so well. There may be a few speakers who do not feel such fear, but it is because they do not know what true speaking is. They have never known the full tide of inspiration which sometimes lifts the orator far above his conceptions, but which first struggles in his own bosom like the pent fires of a volcano. They only come forward to relieve themselves of the interminable stream of twaddle that wells spontaneously to their lips, and can well be spared the pangs preceding the birth of a powerful and living discourse.

This kind of fear belongs to every kind of oratory, but is most intense on those great occasions, in presence of large audiences, when men's passions run high. In mere instructive address, where the ground has been repeatedly gone over and where the effort is mainly of an intellectual character, it is less noticeable. It resembles the awe felt on the eve of all great enterprises, and when excessive, as it is in some highly gifted minds, it constitutes an absolute bar to public speech. But in most cases it is a source of inspiration rather than of repression.

There is a strange sensation often experienced in the presence of an audience. It may proceed from the gaze of the many eyes that turn upon the speaker, especially if he permits himself to steadily return that gaze. Most speakers have been conscious of this in a nameless thrill, a real something, pervading the atmosphere, tangible, evanescent, indescribable. All writers have borne testimony to the power of a speaker's eye in impressing an audience. This influence which we are now considering is the reverse of that picture—the power their eyes may exert upon him, especially before he begins to speak: after the inward fires of oratory are fanned into flame the eyes of the audience lose all terror. By dwelling on the object for which we speak and endeavoring to realize its full importance, we will in a measure lose sight of our personal danger, and be more likely to maintain a calm and tranquil frame of mind.

No change should be made in the plan at the last moment, as that is very liable to produce confusion. This error is often committed. The mind has a natural tendency to go repeatedly over the same ground, revising and testing every point, and it may make changes the consequences of which cannot be in a moment foreseen. But the necessary preparation has been made and we should now await the result calmly and hopefully. Over-study is quite possible, and when accompanied by great solicitude wearies our mind in advance and strips the subject of all freshness. If the eye is fixed too long upon one object with a steadfast gaze, it loses the power to see at all. So the mind, if exerted steadily upon a single topic for a long period, fails in vigor and elasticity at the moment when those qualities are indispensable. That profound thinker and preacher, Frederick W. Robertson, experienced this difficulty and was accustomed to find relief by reading some inspiring paragraphs upon some totally different theme from that he intended to speak about. The energy and enthusiasm of our minds in the moment of speech must be raised to the highest pitch; the delivery of a living discourse is not the dry enumeration of a list of particulars; but we must actually feel an immediate and burning interest in the topics with which we deal. This cannot be counterfeited.

To clearly arrange all thoughts that belong to the subject, lay them aside when the work is done until the moment of speech, and then enter confidently upon them with only such a momentary glance as will assure us that all is right—this is the method to make our strength fully available. This confidence while in waiting seems to the beginner very difficult, but experience rapidly renders it easy. M. Bautain declares that he has been repeatedly so confident in his preparation as to fall asleep while waiting to be summoned to the pulpit!

Those who misimprove the last moments by too much thought and solicitude are not the only class of offenders. Some persons, through mere indolence, suffer the fine lines of preparation which have been traced with so much care to fade into dimness. This error is not unfrequently committed by those who speak a second or third time on the same subject. Because they have once succeeded they imagine that the same success is always at command. No mistake could be greater. It is not enough to have speech-material in a position from which it can be collected by a conscious and prolonged effort, but it must be in the foreground of the mind. There is no time at the moment of delivery for reviving half obliterated lines of memory.

The writer once saw a notable case of failure from this cause. A preacher on a great occasion was much engrossed with other important duties until the hour appointed for his sermon had arrived. With perfect confidence he selected a sketch from which he had preached a short time before and with the general course of which he was no doubt familiar. But when he endeavored to produce his thoughts they were not ready. He became embarrassed, talked at random for a short time, and then had the candor to tell the audience that he could not finish, and to take his seat. Probably half an hour given to reviewing his plan would have made all his previous preparation fresh again, and have spared him the mortification of failure.

In this last interval it is also well to care for the strength and vigor of the body, as its condition greatly influences all mental operations. It is said that the pearl-diver, before venturing into the depths of the sea, always spends a few moments in deep breathing and other bodily preparations. In the excitement of speech, the whirl and hurricane of emotion, it is advisable to be well prepared for the high tension of nerve that is implied. Mental excitement exhausts and wears down the body faster than bodily labor. We must carefully husband our strength that we may be able to meet all demands upon it.

Holyoake makes the following pertinent observation in reference to this point:

"Perhaps the lowest quality of the art of oratory, but one on many occasions of the first importance, is a certain robust and radiant physical health; great volumes of animal heat. In the cold thinness of a morning audience mere energy and mellowness is inestimable; wisdom and learning would be harsh and unwelcome compared with a substantial man, who is quite a housewarming."

Fatiguing and excessive exercise should be very carefully avoided. Holyoake illustrates this from his own experience. He says:

"One Saturday I walked from Sheffield to Huddersfield to deliver on Sunday two anniversary lectures. It was my first appearance there, and I was ambitious to acquit myself well. But in the morning I was utterly unable to do more than talk half inaudibly and quite incoherently. In the evening I was tolerable, but my voice was weak. My annoyance was excessive. I was a paradox to myself. My power seemed to come and go by some eccentric law of its own. I did not find out until years after that the utter exhaustion of my strength had exhausted the powers of speech and thought, and that entire repose, instead of entire fatigue, should have been the preparation for public speaking."

The last statement is somewhat too strong, for absolute rest is not generally advisable. It would leave the speaker, when he began to speak, with languid mind and slowly beating pulse—a state which it would require some minutes for him to overcome. A short, but brisk walk, when the health is good, will invigorate and refresh all his faculties, and often prevent a listless introduction by giving him the vigor to grasp the subject at once and launch right into the heart of it. Should any person doubt the power of exercise to produce this effect, let him, when perplexed with difficult questions in his study, start out over fields and hills, and review the matter in the open air. It is a good thing to carry the breath of the fields into the opening of our addresses.

But when the speaker cannot take this form of exercise in the moments just preceding speech, he may easily find a substitute for it. If alone, he can pace back and forth and swing his arms until the circulation becomes brisk and pours a stream of arterial blood to the brain.

Another simple exercise can be practiced anywhere, and will be of great benefit. Many persons injure themselves by speaking too much from the throat. This is caused by improper, short, and shallow breathing. To breathe properly is beneficial at any time, and does much to prevent or remedy throat and lung disease. But in the beginning of a speech it is doubly important: when once under way, there will be no time to think of either voice or breath: the only safe plan, then, is to have the right mode made habitual and instinctive. This will be greatly promoted if just before beginning we breathe deeply for a few minutes, inflating the lungs to their extremities and sending the warm blood to the very tips of the fingers.

Having now done all we can in advance, nothing remains but to rise and speak. Preparation and precaution are passed. Actual work—the most joyous, thrilling, and spiritual of all human tasks—is now to be entered upon.

CHAPTER XVII

The Introduction

The time for the speech having arrived, we will now consider its separate parts. No division is better for our purpose than that employed in a previous part of this work—a three-fold division into introduction, discussion, and conclusion.

A good introduction is exceedingly valuable, and is to be sought for with great solicitude, if it does not spontaneously present itself. Some kind of an introduction is inevitable, for there will always be a first moment when silence is broken, and our thoughts introduced. The subsiding murmur of the audience tells the speaker that the time of his trial has come. If he is very sensitive, or if he has seldom, if ever, spoken before, his pulse beats fast, his face flushes, and an indescribable feeling of faintness and fear thrills every nerve. He may wish himself anywhere else, but there is now no help for him. He must arise, and for the time stand as the mark for all eyes and the subject of all thoughts.

There is a vast difference between reciting and extemporizing in these opening moments, and the advantage seems to be altogether on the side of recitation. Every word is in its proper place and the speaker may be perfectly calm and self-collected. He is sure that his memory will not fail him in the opening, and encouraged by that assurance, will usually throw his whole power into his first sentences, causing his voice to ring clear and loud over the house.

The extemporizer is in a far more difficult position. He is sure of nothing. The weight of the whole speech rests heavily upon his mind. He is glancing ahead, striving to forecast the coming sentences, as well as carrying forward those gliding over the tongue, and, distracted by this double labor, his first expressions may be feeble and ungraceful.

Yet this modesty and timidity is no real loss: it goes far to conciliate an audience and secure their good-will. We can scarcely fail to distinguish memorized from extemporized discourses by the introduction alone.

To avoid the pain and hesitancy of an unelaborated beginning, some speakers write and memorize the opening passage. This may accomplish the immediate object, but it is apt to be at the expense of all the remainder of the discourse. The mind cannot pass easily from reciting to spontaneous origination; and the voice, being too freely used at first, loses its power. The hearers, having listened to highly polished language, are less disposed to relish the plain words that follow, and the whole speech, which, like the Alpine condor, may have pitched from the loftiest summits, falls fast and far, until the lowest level is reached. A written introduction may be modest and unpretending, but unless it very closely imitates unstudied speech, painful contrasts and disappointments are inevitable.

One mode of avoiding these difficulties is to make no formal introduction, but to plunge at once into the heart of the subject. Sometimes, when the minds of speaker and hearer are already absorbed by the same general topic, as in the midst of a heated political canvass, this mode is very good. Under such circumstances, an interest may soon be aroused which removes all embarrassment. But usually the speaker's mind is full of a subject which is unfamiliar and indifferent to his hearers. It then behooves him to find some mode of gaining their attention and sympathy before he takes the risk of arousing a prejudice against his subject which he might afterward strive in vain to overcome. If something is found which can be made to bear some relation to his subject, without too violent straining, and which already excites interest in their minds, it will be far better to begin with that, and lead them to the proper theme when their attention has been thoroughly aroused.

The introduction should not be left to the chance of the moment. It may often, with great propriety, be prepared after all other parts of the speech are planned. But with even more care than is given to any other portion should the introduction be prearranged. When once the wings of eloquence are fully spread we may soar above all obstructions; but in starting it is well to be assured that the ground is clear about us.

It is only the substance and not the words of the introduction that should be prepared. A single sentence may be mentally forecast, but much beyond would be harmful; and even this sentence should be simple and easily understood. Anything that needs explanation is very much out of place. Neither should the introduction be so striking as to be the part of the discourse longest remembered. Rather than permit the attention to be distracted in that manner, it would be better to have no introduction.

A speaker gains much if he can at the outset arrest the attention and win the sympathy of his hearers and then carry these over to his proper subject. But it may be assumed as certain, that no kind of an apology will accomplish this object—unless, indeed, the speaker is such a favorite that everything in regard to his health or position is an object of deep solicitude to his audience. A popular speaker who happens to be late and apologizes for it by explaining that he had just escaped from a terrible railroad accident would make a good introduction. A loved pastor, in his first sermon after serious illness, might properly begin by talking of his amendment and his joy at addressing Ins flock again. But these are rare exceptions. The speaker about to make any kind of an apology or personal reference as an introduction, may well heed *Punch's advice to persons about to be married:* "Don't."

In many instances it is not easy to get the mere attention of an audience. They come together from many different employments with thoughts engaged upon various topics, and it is difficult to remove distracting influences and fix all minds upon one subject. Sometimes a startling proposition, in the nature of a challenge, will secure the object. Earnestness in the speaker goes far toward it. But above everything else, sameness and monotony must be carefully avoided. When the same audience is frequently addressed, variety becomes essential. The writer knew of a minister who made it a rule to consider the nature, reason, and manner of his subjects, in answer to the supposed questions: "What is it? Why is it? How is it?" The eloquence of Paul could not often have redeemed the faults of such an arrangement.

Some inattention may be expected and patiently borne with at first. Part of the opening words may be lost—an additional reason for not making them of capital importance to the address. It is useless to try by loud tones and violent manner to dispel indifference. If the speaker's words have real weight, and if his manner indicates confidence, one by one the audience will listen, until that electric thrill of sympathy, impossible to describe, but which is as evident to the practiced orator as an accord in music, tells him that every ear is open to his words, and that his thoughts are occupying every mind. Then the orator's power is fully developed, and if himself and his theme are equal to the occasion it is delightful to use that power. This silent, pulsating interest is more to be desired than vehement applause, for it cannot be counterfeited, and it indicates that the heart of the assembly has been reached and melted by the fire of eloquence, and is now ready to be molded into any desired form.

There are two or three general subjects available for introduction which every speaker would do well to study carefully, and which will do much to furnish him with the means of properly approaching his theme. We will mention the most useful of these, premising that no one mode should be depended upon to the exclusion of others.

A good mode of introduction consists in a compliment to an audience. When a truthful and manly compliment can be given it is a most pleasant and agreeable step toward the good-will of those we address; but if used on all occasions indiscriminately, it is meaningless; if transparently false, it is repulsive and disgusting; but when true, there is no reason why it should not be employed.

There are several good introductions of the complimentary character in the 24th and 26th chapters of Acts. When the orator, Tertullus, accused Paul, he began by skillful, but, from the standpoint of his clients, very insincere flattery:

"Seeing that by thee we enjoy great quietness, and that very worthy deeds are done unto this nation by thy providence, we accept it always, and in all places, most noble Felix, with all thankfulness."

No fault can be found with the form of this introduction, but it was untrue, for the men in whose names it was made were the very reverse of thankful to the Roman Governor.

Paul was far too skillful to lose the advantage of beginning his address with a compliment, and too honest to give a false one. There was one fact over which he could rejoice. Felix had been long enough in office to know the ways of his enemies; so Paul uses that as an effective and truthful compliment, while professing his own confidence in his cause.

"Forasmuch as I know that thou hast been for many years a Judge unto this nation, I do the more cheerfully answer for myself, because that thou mayest understand."

In the same exquisite combination of truthfulness and compliment to a bad man, Paul begins his address when before King Agrippa:

"I think myself happy, King Agrippa, because I shall answer for myself this day before thee, touching all the things whereof I am accused of the Jews; especially because I know thee to be expert in all customs and questions which are among the Jews; wherefore, I beseech thee to hear me patiently."

It should always be remembered, however, that compliments, even in the estimation of those complimented, are only grateful in proportion to their judicious character. Their hollowness, if insincere, is easily detected and thoroughly despised.

Effective introductions can also be constructed from those topics of the day which may be supposed to fill all minds. A few words on such subjects, falling in with the general current of thought, may easily lead up to the orator's special topic. The newspapers may thus furnish us, especially while some striking event is yet recent, with the means of arresting the attention of newspaper readers at our first words.

Another good mode of introduction is that of locality. The people of any town may be presumed familiar with the objects or events of interest for which their own place is celebrated. A ludicrous instance of this is narrated of the eloquent Daniel Webster. He had visited Niagara Falls and was to make an oration at Buffalo the same day, but, unfortunately, he sat too long over the wine after dinner. When he arose to speak, the oratorical instinct struggled with difficulties, as he declared, "Gentlemen, I have been to look upon your mag—mag—magnificent cataract, one hundred—and forty—seven—feet high! Gentlemen, Greece and Rome in their palmiest days never had a cataract one hundred—and forty—seven—feet high!"

Another mode of introduction which may be very useful under proper restrictions is that of citing some relevant remark made by an author whose name carries great weight, or so pointed in itself as to at once arrest attention. A great picture, some feature of a landscape, a great historical event, may be cited in the same way. This method of citation is capable of very wide application. If the sentiment or impression made by the citation is directly opposite to that which the speaker wishes to produce this will increase rather than diminish interest, as the enjoyment of contrast and controversy is very keen; but the speaker should feel confident of his ability to overcome the influence of the citation when thus hostile. A favorite introduction to abolition lectures in a former generation was the quotation of some strong and shocking declaration of the rightfulness or beneficence of slavery.

The last mode of introduction we will notice is very similar in character and may be termed that of perception. Something has been seen, heard, or imagined by the speaker, which, because of its simple, tangible character, is easily grasped, and yet leads by some subtle analogy to his topic. He has seen a ragged, desolate boy on the street; he describes that poor fellow to his audience; and then finds them far more ready to listen to a plea for orphan asylums, for education, for better city government, for anything which can have any bearing upon the welfare of the boy.

Here, then, are five principles upon which appropriate introductions may be constructed. Many others might be named, but these cover a wide range and may be very useful. They are:

1. Compliments.
2. Current Events.
3. Local Allusion.
4. Citations.
5. Things seen, heard, or imagined.

A great calamity may come to a speaker from a bad introduction. Speakers who are great in everything else often fail at this point. Some make their introductions too complicated, and thus defeat their own end, as surely as the engineer who gives his railroad such steep grades that no train can pass over it. Others deliver a string of mere platitudes and weary their audience from the beginning.

When from these or other causes our address is misbegun, the consequences may be serious. The thought settles upon the speaker with icy weight that he is failing. This conviction paralyzes all his faculties. He talks on, but grows more and more embarrassed. Incoherent sentences are stammered out which require painful explanation to prevent them from degenerating into perfect nonsense. The outline of his plan dissolves into mist. The points he intended to make which seemed strong and important now look trivial. With little hope ahead he blunders on. The room grows dark before him, and in the excess of his misery he longs for the time when he can close without absolute disgrace. But alas! the end seems far off, and he searches in vain for some avenue of escape. There is none. His throat becomes dry and parched, and command of voice is lost. The audience grow restive, for they are tortured as well as the speaker, and if he were malicious and had time to think about it, he might find some alleviation in that. No one can help him. At length, in sheer desperation, he does what he ought to have done long before—simply stops and sits down—perhaps hurling some swelling morsel of commonplace, as a parting volley, at the audience—bathed in sweat, and feeling that he is disgraced forever! If he is very weak or foolish, he resolves never to speak again without having every word written out before him; if wiser, he only resolves, not only to understand his speech, but how to begin it.

CHAPTER XVIII

Progress of the Speech

The passage from the introduction to the discussion should be made smoothly and gradually. To accomplish this, and to strike the subject at just the right angle, continuing all the interest previously excited, is a most important achievement. A definite object is a great assistance in this part of the work. If the object is clearly in view, we go right up to it with no wasted words, and the people follow our guidance because they see that we are not proceeding at random. But with no strong purpose we are apt to steer about our subject without ever being quite ready to enter upon it. The more brilliant the introduction the more difficult this transition will be. But all these difficulties may be overcome with the aid of a well-constructed plan, and then all the triumphs of oratory are before us.

There is great pleasure in speaking well. An assembly hanging on the words and thinking the thoughts of a single man, gives to him the most subtle kind of flattery. But he must not inhale its fragrance heedlessly, or his fall will be speedy and disastrous. The triumphs of oratory are very fascinating—the ability to sway our fellows at pleasure, to bind them willing captives with the strong chain of our thought—produces a delirious and intoxicating sense of power. But in the best of instances such achievements are very transient, and unless taken advantage of at the moment to work our cherished purposes, the opportunity is lost. Even during a single address it is hard to maintain the influence of a happy moment. Speakers sometimes utter a great and noble thought and the nameless thrill of eloquence is felt, but some irrelevant phrase or commonplace sentiment dissolves the charm. To avoid this, the whole discourse must be animated with some controlling purpose, and in its general character, tend upward, until its close.

The law of climax ought to be carefully considered by the speaker. There may be more than one culmination of interest in an address, separated by an interval less absorbing and powerful, but this decline should only be allowed in order to prepare a second or third climax grander than all before. To violate this rule and have a speech "flatten out" toward its close, is a fearful error. Better reduce the length of the whole by one-half or three-fourths, and maintain interest and attention to the end.

A few miscellaneous considerations in regard to the style and manner of the speech may be inserted here as well as anywhere.

Diffuseness is often supposed to be a necessary quality of extemporaneous speech. Many speakers do fall into it, but they need not. They are diffuse because they are unwilling or unable to say exactly what they mean, but come near it, and continue their efforts until they are satisfied. They furnish no clear view of any idea, but only a kind of twilight illumination. This serious fault may be overcome in spontaneous speech as readily as in writing. He who thinks clearly and forcibly will talk in the same manner. Exquisite finish and elaborate verbal arrangement are not to be looked for in off-hand speech, but each idea may be expressed with great force, vigor, and accuracy of shading.

This ability to say precisely what we mean in few words, and at the first effort, constitutes one of the great beauties of a spoken style. The hearer is filled with grateful surprise when some new and living idea is suddenly placed before him clothed in a single word or sentence. A diffuse speaker gives so many premonitions of his thought that the audience have guessed it, and may even come to believe that they have always known it, before he has made his formal presentment. Of course, they are wearied, and never give him credit for an original conception.

If troubled with this fault, frequently forecast what to say; drive it into the smallest number of vivid, expressive words; then, without memorizing the language, reproduce the same thought briefly in the hurry of speech. If not successful in making it as brief as before, repeat the effort. This exercise will, in time, give the ability to condense. But to exercise it the temptation to fine language must be overcome. No sentence should be introduced for mere glitter or sparkle: a single unnecessary word may require others to justify or explain it, and thus may ruin a whole discourse. The danger of showy language in speech is far greater than in writing, for if the writer be drawn too far away from his subject he can strike out the offending sentences and begin again, while the speaker has but one trial. If beauty lies in his way, well; but if not, he should never abandon his course to seek it.

We have seen many directions for "expanding thought," and have heard young speakers admire the ease and grace of such expansion. But thoughts are not like medicines which require dilution to be more palatable. It is better to give the essence of an idea and go on to something else. There should be clear and ample expression; condensation carried to the point of obscurity would be a fault; but nothing more than clearness is needed. If thoughts are few it is better to delve for others rather than to attenuate and stretch what we have.

A popular error exists as to the kind of language best adapted to the purposes of oratory. High-sounding epithets and Latinized words are considered the fitting medium of speech. These may overawe ignorant hearers, but can never strike the chords of living sympathy which bind all hearts together. If we use terms hard to be understood the effort put forth by hearers to master their meaning is just so much subtracted from the force of the address. The homely Saxon words that dwell on the lips of the people will unload their wealth of meaning in the heart as soon as the sound strikes the ear. Uncommon words build a barrier around thought; familiar ones are like a railroad over which it glides swiftly to its destination.

All debased and slang words should be rejected, unless the speech is to partake of the nature of burlesque: we do not advocate "the familiarity that breeds contempt:" this is also a hurtful extreme. The two great requisites in the use of words are that they should exactly express our ideas, and that they should be familiar: the charms of melody and association are not to be despised, but they are secondary.

Every speech should have its strong points, upon which especial reliance is placed. A skillful general has his choice battalions reserved to pierce the enemy's line at the decisive moment, and win the battle. In both the physical and the mental contest, it is important to place these reserves aright that all their weight may be felt.

A crisis occurs in nearly all living addresses—a moment in which a strong argument or a fervid appeal will accomplish our purpose—just as a vigorous charge, or the arrival of reinforcements, will turn the doubtful scale of battle. The speaker, from the opening of his speech, should have his object clearly in view and drive steadily toward it, and when within reach, put forth his whole power in a mighty effort, achieving the result for which the whole speech was devised. If the right opportunity is neglected it seldom returns, and an hour's talk may fail to accomplish as much as one good burning sentence thrown in at the right time. Much talk after the real purpose of an address is accomplished also is useless and even perilous.

It has all along been taken for granted that the speaker has something worthy to say. Without this a serious address deserves no success, although under some circumstances nothing but sound to tickle the ears is desired. Such speeches are well enough in their way, but they rank with the performances on the piano by which a young lady entertains her uncritical visitors. They cannot be called speeches in any real sense. The fact that a speaker has a solid and worthy foundation of knowledge and an adequate purpose gives him confidence. He knows that if his words are not instinct with music, and if the pictures of his fancy are not painted in the brightest colors, he has yet a just claim upon the attention of his hearers.

It is not necessary that the orator's thoughts should be exceedingly profound; the most vital truths lie near the surface, within reach of all. But most men do not dwell long enough upon one subject to master its obvious features, and when some one does fully gather up and fairly present what belongs to a worthy theme it is like a new revelation. A good illustration of this is found in the sublimity Dean Stanley imparts to the story of the Exodus of Israel. Few new facts are presented, but these are so arranged and vivified by a thoughtful mind that the subject glows into new meaning. The extemporaneous speaker may have abundant time for such study of every topic within his range of addresses, and if he uses it aright, he can soon wield a charm far beyond any jingling combination of words.

When an orator stands before an audience, shall he expect to overwhelm them by his eloquence? Such a result is possible but not probable; and it can never be safely calculated upon. If persons attempt to be greatly eloquent on all occasions, they are apt to end by becoming ridiculous. Good sense and solid usefulness are better objects of endeavor.

Any man who studies a subject until he knows more about it than his neighbors can interest them in a fireside explanation, if they care for the subject at all: he tells his facts in a plain style and is understood. Many persons will listen delighted to a man's conversation until midnight, but will fall asleep in ten minutes if he tries to make a speech to them. In the first case he talks, and is simple and unaffected; in the other he speaks and feels that he must use a style stiffened up for the occasion.

When Henry Clay was asked how he became so eloquent, he said that he could tell nothing about it; all he knew was that when he commenced an address he had only the desire to speak what he had prepared (not memorized), and adhered to this line of preparation until he was enwrapped in the subject, and carried away, he knew not how. This was a good course, for if the extraordinary inspiration did not come, a good and sensible speech was secured at any rate.

Some of these considerations may be of service if weighed in advance, but when the speaker once ascends the platform he must rely on his own tact for the management of all details. Closely observing the condition of the audience, and taking advantage of every favoring element, he moves steadily toward his object. With an unobstructed road before him, which he has traveled in thought until it is familiar, he will advance with ease and certainty. As he looks upon interested faces, new ideas arise, and if fitting, are woven into harmony with previous preparations, often with thrilling effect. Each emotion enkindled by sympathy embodies itself in words that move the heart as prepared language could not do, and each moment his own conviction sinks deeper into the hearts of his hearers.

There are three principal ways of concluding a speech. One of the most graceful is to condense a clear view of the whole argument and tendency of the address into a few words, and leave the summing up thus made to produce its own effect. Discourses aiming principally to produce conviction may very well be concluded in this manner. To throw the whole sweep of an argument, every point of which has been previously elaborated, into a few telling sentences will contribute powerfully to make the impression permanent.

Another and very common mode is to close with an application or with practical remarks. When the address is a sermon, this form of closing is frequently termed an exhortation, and the whole speech is made to bear upon the duty of the moment. The conclusion should be closely connected with the remainder of the address: if it be so general in character as to fit any speech it will be of little service to any.

A conclusion should always be short and contain no new matter. Few things are more disastrous than the practice of drawing toward an end and then launching out into a new discussion. All good things that have been said, all previous favorable impressions, are obliterated by this capital fault. We should be careful to finish the discussion of our theme before we indicate that the conclusion has been reached. And if, at the moment of finishing, we happen to think of anything, however vital, which has been omitted, it had better be left to another time and place altogether.

A third method of closing is to simply break off when the last item is finished. The full development of the discourse is thus made its ending, care being taken that the last item discussed shall be of weight and dignity. This is by no means the easiest form of conclusion, but rightly managed it is one of the most effective.

CHAPTER XIX

AFTER THE SPEECH

When a fervent and successful discourse has been concluded there comes a feeling of inexpressible relief. The burden of an important speech rests with accumulating force upon the mind from the time the subject is chosen until it becomes well-nigh intolerable. When speech actually begins every power is called into play and exerted to its utmost capacity. The excitement of the conflict hurries the speaker on, and although he may not at the time realize the gigantic exertions put forth, yet when he pauses at length, perhaps exhausted, but with the victory won, the sense of rest, relief, and security, is exceedingly delightful.

After such an effort both mind and body do need rest. There are speakers who profess to feel no fatigue after an hour's labor, but these are seldom in the front rank of orators. If the soul has been aroused and all the man's faculties bent to the accomplishment of a great purpose, relaxation is often followed by a sense of utter prostration. Nothing better for the moment can be advised than to abandon one's self to the luxury of utter repose. Social intercourse and all distractions should as far as possible be avoided. If circumstances permit, a short sleep, if but for a few minutes, will afford great relief; and in most cases sleep will come if wisely courted.

After resting, it is well to ponder closely the lessons derived from each new experience in speaking. To indulge in exultation over success or to lament over failure is not profitable. The speaker is not a perfect judge of either. He has probably done the best he could at the time, and there the case should rest, except so far as he sees the need or the means of future improvement.

But judgment of success or failure cannot easily be avoided. If the speaker's standard is low, he may pass beyond it without accomplishing anything worthy of high praise: or if he is despondent in nature he may have expected little and may now feel correspondingly elated because he has exceeded his very moderate expectations. But it is a curious fact that speakers are often least pleased with their best speeches. In the mightiest efforts of the mind the standard is placed very high—perhaps beyond the possibility of attainment—and the speaker works with his eyes fixed upon that summit, and probably, after all his exertions, sees it shining still far above him. His ideas are but half expressed; he is mortified that there should be such a difference between conception and realization. But his hearers have been led over untrodden fields of thought, and knowing nothing of the grander heights still above the orator's head, they are naturally filled with enthusiasm, and cannot enter into the feelings of the speaker if he is foolish enough to tell them of his disappointment.

This is the reason that we are least able to judge of the success of speeches that have been long meditated and thoroughly prepared. The subject expands as we study, its outlines becoming grander and vaster until they pass beyond our power of adequate representation. Each separate thought in the whole discussion that is fully mastered becomes familiar, and is not, therefore, valued at its true worth. Sometimes, when we begin to speak with little thought, intending to give only easy and common views of the subject, everything appears fresh before us, and if some striking ideas arise, their novelty gives them three-fold value, and we imagine that we have made a great speech. All this constitutes no argument against diligent preparation, but it should stimulate us to bring up our powers of expression more nearly to the level of our conceptions.

There should never be extreme discouragement over an apparent failure. Some good end may be reached even by a very poor speech. One evening the writer preached when weary and almost unprepared. From first to last the effort was painful, and to prevent absolute failure the intended plan had to be abandoned, and detached thoughts from any source thrown in. Yet that discourse, which was scarcely worthy of the name, elicited warmer approval and did more apparent good than any one preached for several previous months. One or two fortunate illustrations redeemed every defect, so far as the audience (but not the speaker) was concerned.

Whatever judgment we may entertain of our own performances, it is not usually wise to tell our hearers, or to ask their opinions. Criticisms spontaneously offered need not be repulsed, but all seeking for commendation is childish or disgusting. It is sweet to hear our efforts praised, and most of men can bear an amount of flattery addressed to themselves which would be insufferable if offered to others; but this disposition, if much indulged, becomes ungovernable and exposes us to well-deserved ridicule. It is pitiable to see a man who has been uttering wise and eloquent words afterward stooping to beg crusts of indiscriminating flattery from his hearers.

Whenever there is a probability that any discourse will be repeated, it is well to review it soon after delivery, while its impression is still fresh upon the mind, and if any defect appears, amend it in the plan, and add to the same plan all the valuable ideas that have been suggested during the speech or afterward. In this manner we keep each discourse up to the high watermark of our ability.

Some orators are accustomed to write their speeches out in full after delivery. When the theme is important and time permits, this is a good exercise, but in many—perhaps the majority of cases—the labor would outweigh the profit.

No such objection applies to reviewing and correcting a verbatim report of our speeches. To many speakers such a review of the exact words they have uttered would be a striking and not altogether pleasing revelation. Pet phrases, which might otherwise be unnoticed for years; faults of expression, and especially the profuseness of words, in which extemporaneous speakers are tempted to indulge;—would all be forced upon our notice. We would be surprised to learn that we could often write the discourse in one-fourth the words employed in delivery. To form the habit of thus condensing our speeches after delivery would have a powerful tendency toward compacting thought in speech itself. The only hindrance in applying this capital means of improvement consists in the difficulty of obtaining such shorthand reports. Where this cannot be overcome a part of the advantage may be gained by taking the plan and from it writing out the same kind of a compact presentation of the thoughts as uttered. This differs from writing in full by making no effort to record exact words or forms of expression, but only to recall from memory and from the sketch the exact thoughts that were expressed in the language of the moment. Even if the same kind of brief sketch has been made previous to the act of speech, this does not take the place of what we now recommend; for the former outline may have been greatly modified by the experience of delivery.

In whatever form the best result of the discourse is recorded, great care should be taken in its preservation. The plan, sketch, or fully written discourse may be slipped into an envelope (which may also contain all illustrative scraps, notes, or references to books that bear upon the discourse) and on the back may be written the title, time, and character of delivery, with any other facts of importance. If the young speaker will faithfully follow up such a method of recording the results of his oratorical experience, he will find it one of the best forms of discipline, and the record itself—carefully indexed, frequently reviewed, and kept within reasonable bulk—will in time possess a value greater than gold.